WAR AND DEATH

OF THE

AMERICAN DREAM

WAR AND DEATH OF THE AMERICAN DREAM

Robert Thomas Raming

MOUNTAIN OF LIGHT PUBLISHING
2530 Vista Way # F306
Oceanside, CA 92054

Manufactured in the United States of America

10 9 8 7 6 5 4 3 2 1

Library of Congress # 2005920588

ISBN 0-9656382-4-3

Raming, Robert Thomas
War and Death of the American Dream

DEDICATED TO

Jeannette Rankin, the first woman elected to Congress and the only member of Congress to vote "No" to both World War I and World War II

and

My sisters, Joanna and Marianne,
for their love, strength, and courage.

TABLE OF CONTENTS

PREFACE

The world has produced its share of visionaries, but none have been more correct in their assessment of the future than Aldous Huxley. I first read his book *Brave New World* in 1962. It is an utterly futuristic tale about a government gone way beyond wrong. I marveled at his ideas and wondered where he could have come up with such an inspiration, convinced that such a reality was entirely a work of science fiction.

Yet as I look around me today, with the advent of nano-technology and Viagra, I am dumbfounded by the realization that his work of fiction could become a reality in my lifetime. The current popular dogma postulates that if the government can offer each individual an equal opportunity for success, than it will be able to socially engineer a better world. This can be classified under the heading *The Government Thinks It Can Improve on God's Imperfections.*

But how can the government equalize such intangibles as motivation, desire, persistence, determination, or courage? At the beginning of the 21st century, our government has involved itself in almost every aspect of our lives, and not for the better. Either our government has become extremely incompetent, or there is an ulterior motive behind the intentional mismanagement of the U.S. government. Both scenarios should give the American people grave cause for concern.

We are the richest, most creative, most powerful nation that has ever existed. But our national debt is about to strangle us, our institutions of education and health care are crumbling, border security is being ignored at what might be the most critical period in our history, and we are fighting a war that could last 50 years. Could Iraq be our Waterloo?

If our government is being mismanaged because of greed, incompetence, corruption, or addiction, then we need to make immediate changes in the political system that is making a mess of things. If there is an ulterior motive behind what appears to be the intentional destruction of the American way of life, then the trouble is even more serious.

The latter alternative, that an intentional effort is being made to subvert our liberty, means that the American Dream is on the verge of extinction—which means that the power and sophistication of the Puppet Masters is way beyond anything imagined by the American people. The marketing mechanisms employed by this shadow society have been embedded deeply into our psyche.

Our Founding Fathers were more worried about America surrendering from within to the tyranny of human nature than about our conquest by foreign enemies. I am in awe of their wisdom and insight, for their worst fears may indeed be coming to pass. The decline of our institutions and identity over the last half-century is accelerating at a rapid pace.

Each American has their own unique understanding of the American Dream, but at its core there is a shared similarity. As a nation of immigrants based on specific ideals, we hold liberty close to our hearts: liberty from the tyranny of political maniacs and government, from slavery, from the notion that women are second-class citizens. Liberty is at the very heart of the American Dream, for it is the beacon of light responsible for all of the greatness America has achieved.

George Washington might be called the original liberator. All those who have followed in his path are cheap imitations offering useless propaganda and worthless dogma. Their intent has not been to liberate or enlighten but to subvert and control. My concern is that the very forces of human nature that concerned our Founding Fathers are now destroying America. They designed a minimalist government to prevent just such a fate, but even their wisdom may prove insufficient!

There can be no doubt but that the greatness of America is in serious decline, and if our desire for liberty and freedom has declined, then that is how it should be. But if the responsibility lies in the hands of our leaders because of their greed, intoxication, or stupidity, then it is a problem we must address, no matter how difficult. However, if there is another reason, a darker and more sinister force at work here, then we must realize it now. For the time to save our Republic is slipping away, and the evil force we are confronting is much stronger than most of us realized. Aldous Huxley was way ahead of his time, but his warnings live on. He understood what Edmund Burke proclaimed in 1784, "The people never give up their liberties but under some illusion." If we do nothing, the international prayer of the 21st century might become, *Oh Lord, please save us from this Brave New World Order.*

INTRODUCTION

I have written this book with the women of America in mind, for they are mother to us all, and our future may lie in their hands. The anger and hatred of the 2004 election was so extreme that it oftentimes obscured the issues and the fact that as Americans, we have much more in common than is usually acknowledged. I believe the politicians were responsible for much of the bitterness and animosity that carried the day. And it seems that with a war being waged and our soldiers once again coming home dead and wounded, we need to rethink our priorities and establish a new direction for the future of American.

When I was in high school it was understood that it was a man's world. That euphemism had been valid, to a large extent, for most of the history of mankind. But that has changed, and women are now taking their rightful position in our society. This did not happen because our Founding Fathers set out to make it so, but because they established a system of government unlike anything previously known before. We can say that the liberation of women has been the by-product of a system designed to allow for the maximum expression of liberty, that we might achieve excellence as we pursue our creative potential.

Some would say that advancing technology is really responsible for the liberation of American women, and to some extent this is also true, but only because our Founding Fathers established a form of government dedicated to liberty and the rights of the individual. Our philosophical foundation was designed to stimulate a free and competitive environment that would reward achievement and excellence.

The by-product of this system of government is that it allows us to express as much vitality and creativity as we possibly can. In the process we ended slavery, not because that was our forefathers' intention, but because it was the natural course of our Constitution and Bill of Rights. The difference between permission and coercion is the difference between liberty and bondage. Speaking of coercion, along the course of our expansion we were most unkind to the Native peoples already here. Recent attempts to give the Native Americans compensation in the form of casino rights does not excuse our past, but it does speak to our sense of justice and fair play.

As a student during the Vietnam War I protested against the decisions of my government. At that time I never doubted that America was my home, although I was hopeful that my generation could change the foreign policies that had committed us to the war.

The 21st century finds the American woman with more freedom and choices than have ever been experienced in any nation. Again, this has been the result of a system of government dedicated to the highest expression of liberty and justice the world has ever seen. And now, more than ever, we need her intuition and wisdom to help us navigate our way through a most difficult set of challenges that threaten to destroy us.

The history of mankind has been one of constant warfare and brutality. The male was designed to be a warrior, a fighter, a protector, and has always been expendable. Yet our Founding Fathers were good students of history, and they strongly admonished us to stay out of the politics and wars of other nations. Yet we have failed to heed their warning. Is that because the male psyche has been unable to radically change its nature in such a short time? Or have there been other forces at work designed to keep us engaged in foreign politics and wars? For there is no doubt that by the early 20th century we had totally disregarded the wisdom of our founders and were eager to compete with the Europeans for an empire.

Our primary difference from the Europeans when it came to empire building was that we had plenty of land, and so we were more concerned with exporting the ideology upon which we were founded. We were the first nation built upon a set of ideals, and that has defined us to this day. However, the 20th century provides ample evidence that our aggressive tendencies still define us to a large extent, and now more than ever we need to find a balance that will sustain us through this century and beyond.

This is one of the reasons women are so important to our survival. Their status as equals in the decision making process cannot be denied, and we will need the courage of their open hearts and their desire for truth to balance the male ego and our tendency to seek security by means of physical strength and our dominating technology. The dark secrets about our involvement in the wars of the 20th century paint an ugly picture, and some people may find them hard to believe. But only by acknowledging the mistakes of our past leaders will we be able heal the wounds and move on. Only then will we be able to chart a clear and straight course for tomorrow.

Our foreign policy can no longer be determined by large egos thumping their chest and chanting simple slogans of freedom and democracy. We have to build a secure defense for the nation that we love, and make clear, realistic decisions about how to maximize our strengths to survive the challenges ahead. Using just half of our potential would be to short-change all Americans, and we cannot afford that.

The decisions ahead will be difficult ones. We need new leaders of courage who can look into the face of fear and lies and remain resolute in their search for the truth. The last century saw too many American soldiers come home in body bags for no good reason, yet once again we are sacrificing the best and the brightest to the coffin.

I am going to make the case for Neutrality *(which does not mean isolation!)*, that we have fought too many wars for no other reason than to serve the egos of our leaders and to line the pockets of the military industrial complex. The threat that faces us today is not only the threat of constant warfare over the next 50 years, but the decline and decay of America itself. Our demise will not be sudden, but will happen slowly, just as the tide comes in and erodes the shoreline. Our foundations are rotting through to the core, and the future of America hangs in the balance.

Our ability to rebuild America may well be determined by our ability to stay out of foreign conflicts. The women that I know who have children or will have children in the years ahead may be those best qualified to decide whether the case I present is a valid one. I am counting on the women of America, who want all of our sons and daughters to achieve the American Dream, to lead us boldly into the future.

Now that we have been physically violated here at home for the first time, we have to ask ourselves what policy will best guarantee the survival and success of America. What choices do we have? What changes can we agree to that will stack the odds in our favor? I hope that the ideas presented here will appeal to the intelligent, pragmatic minds of both men and women. It is imperative that we consider all of our options; it is vital that we learn from our past mistakes.

Someone once said that those who don't learn from history are condemned to repeat it. Yet one of our critical issues is the state of our educational system. American history has been relegated to a secondary status, and our children are fairly ignorant of the principles upon which America was founded. I know that there is a part of the population who believe that the Declaration of Independence and the Constitution are out of date and irrelevant, but I would disagree. How will our children be able to make intelligent decisions about the future if they don't understand how we got to where we are?

This nation was founded by men and women of wisdom and courage. We know the stories of some of them, such as Washington,

Jefferson, and Franklin, and history has taught us that they were not perfect. Like many of us, they had their flaws. But like them, we have to rise above our flaws and discover the eternal truths that bind us. For nothing less than the liberty and freedoms of America is at stake.

We have to rediscover our common heritage, which is more than where we were born. It is the free spirit of liberty, the courage to face our fears, the freedom to express our dreams, and the ability to find a balance that has sustained us for over 200 years. These were all by-products of our Constitution and Bill of Rights. Our Founding Fathers considered carefully the ideas and principles upon which this nation was founded, they wrote them down simply, and then they fought for them bravely.

As a student of history I have studied great nations of the past. I have read of the wars they fought in distant lands while their liberties and freedoms were slowly sacrificed in the name of government, God, and glory. The fight America is engaged in right now is far greater than that being fought with bombs and bullets. It is being waged right here, for the hearts and minds of all Americans. It is a fight for the truth, for what our politicians have not been telling us. Their politics of hate, anger, fear, power, greed and jealously have obscured what is taking place beneath the surface, a truth they don't want you to discover.

We need those individuals whose hearts and minds are dedicated to preserving this way of life to come forward now, to help us overcome the obstacles that confront us. The words and ideas of our forefathers, profound in their wisdom, are being attacked and defiled from within, and misunderstood by many.

We have not always done right, but we have tried to do our best. If you believe there is the potential for some kind of Utopia here on earth, you may not enjoy this book. But if you will acknowledge that nowhere in the history of mankind has there been an effort more dedicated to truth, justice, and the creative pursuit of excellence, than this should prove a worthwhile experience for you.

In the pages that follow I will examine the major issues that threaten our future, such as immigration, the budget deficit, the corruption of our political leaders and the war on terror. I hope that all of you will open your hearts to the problems that divide us and dig deeply into the truth, for if we are not capable of creating a future based on honesty and neutrality, we may have to defend America with the blood and bones of those we cherish most dearly—our sons and our daughters.

It is not too late, but our downfall is progressing rapidly, and most of us are only vaguely aware of this fact. We, as a people, have the courage, intelligence, and creative abilities to restore the luster, hope and promise that has made America great. If we can find some common ground, if we can recognize the gift we have been given, if we can appreciate our differences yet honor that which unites us, it is possible that we might build something very special. But we have to do it together. And we have to do it now.

We the people have to stand up and take a very serious and honest look at what is going on in our government. We have to educate ourselves, independent of what the political demigods and spin-doctors say. We have to choose a new direction for the future based on the ideals of justice and liberty our Founding Fathers worked so hard to create. I honor those who have gone before me, those who teach me today, and those brilliant hearts and minds that will keep the light of liberty and freedom burning brightly.

Because of the benefit of technology and the numerous events of political importance that will be happening between the time I am writing this and the date of publication, I will publish the final chapter of this book on my web site, www.uniteamericanow.com. It is imperative that we broaden the discussion and include as many of our family and friends as possible. I hope that together we can build a better America.

PART I

If my sons did not want war, there would be none.

—Gutle Schnapper Rothschild
wife of Mayer Rothschild and mother to their five sons

I have ever deemed it fundamental for the United States, never to take active part in the quarrels of Europe. Their political interests are entirely distant from ours. Their mutual jealousies, their balance of power, their complicated alliances, their forms and principles of government, are all foreign to us. They are nations of eternal war.

—Thomas Jefferson

1

HONOR AMONG THIEVES

There is a dark cloud on the horizon, an evil, ominous cloud that threatens to devour America as we know it today. Spawned during the European Dark Ages, it cut its teeth on the Crusades and has evolved into a diabolical presence determined to destroy our most sacred possessions, the Declaration of Independence and the United States Constitution. To begin to recognize this devious demon, we need to understand from whence it came. To defeat it, we will have to become aware of how it thrives amongst us today.

For many years after its fall, the Holy Roman Empire left a formidable impression in the minds of most Europeans. In fact, many Europeans became obsessed with the idea of recreating their own empires after the fall of Rome. The Russian word Czar and the German word Kaiser both mean Caesar. And Napoleon had himself crowned emperor.

The Roman Empire was characterized by a unified and strong central government that ruled with an iron fist, and those in power felt free to change the laws as the situation demanded. They could get away with this because it was claimed that the emperor was descended from the gods. Kings were chosen by a group of wise men reputed to have the ability to commune with the gods; these wise men were called augurs.

The augurs then gave the king magical powers. He was inaugurated much as our President is today.

The underlying premise of the Roman government was that it could do whatever it saw fit to promote the interests of the Empire. This is the basis of fascism. It is easy to see why many people believe that political power is the game of playing God. The golden period of Rome, known as the Pax Romana, lasted for about two hundred years, beginning in 31 B.C. By 500 A.D. the Dark Ages had fallen over Europe, a time so filled with poverty and bloodshed that many longed for the return of the Roman Empire.

It was during these Dark Ages that the feudal lords established themselves as a sort of royalty. Yet they were no more than thugs who controlled almost every aspect of the lives of the peasants who lived on their property. At the bottom of society's ladder, considered chattel of the feudal lords, these serfs were consumed by misery and poverty.

Until the early 1300s, learning and science were considered heresy and could land one in the hands of the Inquisition, created by the Catholic Church. The Church held sway over the peasants, and to some extent over the feudal lords as well, even as they were establishing themselves as kings and divine rulers. The church and the kings share a long history in their struggle for power and wealth.

A fourth group emerged during these times, an alliance of secret societies, one of which was known as the Knights Templar. Entry into these groups was limited to a select few, the primary prerequisites being breeding and wealth. These underground organizations survived by their cunning and connections, eluding the taxes and control of kings. Their trade was often of a very unsavory sort, consisting of smuggling, drugs, and slaves.

The kings often warred among themselves for power and land, and the serfs were taxed to raise the necessary finances to support these ventures. But war did bring opportunity, for enlisting in the Crusades offered adventure over the drudgery of serfdom, as well as the possibility of bettering one's circumstances. Becoming a mercenary or going to sea as a pirate offered similar possibilities, though they risked prosecution on their return. Crusaders, pirates and mercenaries all looked forward to returning home with enough treasure to live out the rest of their days.

Both mercenary and pirate became members of a society within a society, and save for the possibility of death they lived better than the sailors of the British Navy and were treated less harshly. They banded together by covenants that provided protection from British Naval law, and every sailor aboard voted on these secret pledges. As Steven Sora writes in *Secret Societies of America's Elite*, these were the first instances of the one-man, one-vote system of democratic rule, a system that would not be duplicated until the American Constitution. The pirates avoided the rigid Navy class structure, and their widowed and wounded were usually better cared for as well.

This was because the booty they plundered was shared equally among the crew. The captain was chosen by popular vote, and he would get a double share, while the first assistant would get a share and a half. These extra portions were granted based on ability, and if the captain failed to live up to the task at hand he would be relieved of duty. This was totally contrary to the policy of the British Navy, where the crew received a minimal wage and most of the wealth went to the king.

To deal with conventional society, these secret organizations had to have connections. Not only did they have to be able to depend on each other for their lives, but to land their ships safely in a given port and to sell their ill-gotten goods they needed alliances that could be trusted. This meant a brotherhood that went deep and was well organized. Secret oaths, codes, and handshakes became the signals that someone could be trusted, that they were part of an underground network that would provide food, lodging, and information that was often above the law. Thus the expression "honor among thieves."

When Pope Urban sanctioned the Crusades as holy in 1093, an alliance was struck with these secret groups to take back the Holy Land from the Muslims. This was the unofficial beginning of an unholy alliance between the Catholic Church and the secret societies, such as the Knights Templar, that would flourish. They developed as an order of fighting monks whose loyalty to the Roman pope was often in word only, for their primary aim was to enrich themselves.

While the Knights Templar was becoming the vanguard of Europe's military they also established themselves in other industries, such as property management and shipbuilding. They became immensely wealthy, pirating and plundering as they went. They were able to get around the church's usury laws, and the Templar bank established the world's first banking system. Their clients included kings and royalty. The church even declared that the state should not tax the Crusaders or the estates of the Order, making it easy for them to avoid feudal taxation. At one time they owned 9,000 houses throughout Europe, their wealth and power equaling that of the kings.

The Knights Templar and the rival Christian Order of the Knights of Malta cornered the slave trade in the Holy Lands. There all slaves were called Muslims, no matter their religion, because the pope in Rome had banned Christian slaves in the kingdom of Jerusalem. Muslims who wanted to become Christians were denied.

In 1307 the French king attempted to break up the Knights Templar, as he owed them a lot of money. They got word of the impending raid, and most were able to escape with their lives and their treasure. This forced the secret societies to go deeper underground. Splinter groups were established in Scotland, Spain, Portugal, and other areas throughout Europe.

The backlash against the power and wealth of the Roman Catholic Church predates the Reformation, but the bitterness of the Inquisition, excess taxation, and numerous wars also divided the Knights Templar and their successors. The Scottish group remained Catholic, while in France most became Protestant. The religious wars of the times often pitted one group against another. Nonetheless, with their international military force, their religious connections, and their widespread financial interests and businesses, the Knights Templar became the world's first multinational corporation.

There was another organization that came into being during this time that would also wield enormous power. This was the House of Rothschild, which came to prominence during the 1770s in Europe. Mayer Rothschild was a master of finance who sent his five sons to the capitols of Western Europe, where they went into the business of finance. The Rothschilds always acted as a single entity and became very successful as international financiers. At the same time Mayer also established the most effective intelligence operation known to man (the forerunner of our CIA).

It was at this time that Mayer financed a secret society that would become known as the Illuminati. They infiltrated French Freemasonry and began to foment a rebellion in France to run up the nation's debt and at the same time extinguish some of the Rothschild competitors. In the book *Descent into Slavery,* Des Griffin quotes Sir Walter Scott as saying that the Illuminati planned the French Revolution.

Among his many enterprises, it was quite common for Mayer to finance both sides of the wars in Europe, as he did in Napoleon's battle against the British at Waterloo. With the advantage of his sophisticated spy network, he was able to discover the outcome of the Battle of Waterloo earlier than anyone else at the London Stock Exchange, to his benefit. Mayer spread a rumor that the British had lost, which caused their bonds to become almost worthless. He bought them for pennies on the dollar. When news of the British victory reached the Exchange, his profits skyrocketed in value.

The Americas represented tremendous opportunity for the Rothschilds and the massive European organizations of the Knights Templar, who were able to maintain most of their power behind the scenes as they became active in the New World. The influence of the Knights Templar touched the lives of almost all Americans. Rooted in the Masonic lodge system and the Freemasonry, Benjamin Franklin acknowledged that success in the printing business depended on which lodge one belonged to.

By the time the secret societies reached America, the Freemasons had split into two organizations, one that catered to the men of the trades, or guilds, and the other for the more educated and wealthy members of power and influence. Some were able to participate in both groups, though this was rare. Such an individual was John Hancock, famous for his smuggling. By the time of the Revolution he employed a large portion of the workers in New England.

The lodges of the ruling elite were few and very secretive, keeping almost no written records. This is important because this pattern of an elite few wielding power behind the scenes and pulling the strings is still their modus operandi in the 21st century.

George Washington was a Mason, and the nation's capitol was based on Masonic architecture. Approximately 40 of the signatures on the Constitution were those of Masons. A large part of Franklin's success in getting the French to help in the Revolutionary War was due to his ability to mingle freely among the Masons of Paris.

Many of our Founding Fathers were slave owners, smugglers, and drug runners. As Sora points out, the family wealth of Franklin and Theodore Roosevelt was built on the profits from the slave trade and smuggling opium into China. Ulysses S. Grant married into an opium smuggling family with ties to America and Europe. The first families of New York and New England provided funding for the founding of such institutions as Harvard, Yale, Brown, and Princeton with money earned in the slave and drug trades. Both of the Bush Presidents and Senator Kerry belonged to the same Skull and Bones Club at Yale that was funded with money from the China trade.

Some of the wealthiest families on the East Coast owe their fortunes to the illegal smuggling of drugs and slaves. These include the Pillsbury, Astor, Forbes, Brown, Delano, Sassoon, Appleton, Cabot, Lowell, and Lodge families, to name just a few. The money they earned illegally was often reinvested in companies that have become American institutions, such as Chase Manhattan Bank and Boston's Fleet Financial Bank. The power and wealth of these families has grown to even greater proportions in today's society.

These secret societies have shed their criminal past, going to great lengths to hide this information, and a wealthy few have become what I refer to as the Global Elite. Their influence often hides behind the corporate giants that populate the globe, and their long-felt influence on American history is stronger than ever. Sora suggests that the secrecy and connections employed in accumulating these fortunes are still at work today, and that they are even more powerful than in the past.

2

A REVOLUTION OF HEART AND MIND

As we have seen, Europe was taken over by feudal lords who were nothing more than cutthroats and thugs. They set up small kingdoms with a castle in the center and treated everyone who lived on or near their land as personal property. These feudal lords taxed, killed, and regulated their serfs as they saw fit. These Dark Ages were a time of endless misery and starvation.

To establish order, the people generally relied on the most trusted person in the community to solve personal disputes. This was usually a member of the clergy. Some of the clergy made a career out of hearing disputes and settling cases, and they became judges. In order to avoid religious conflict, these judges eventually distilled the basic law down to two principles that were common to all religions. In his book *Whatever Happened to Justice?*, Richard Maybury sums up the essence of these two laws:

> 1. Do all you have agreed to do. (Maybury explains that this is the basis for what we know as contract law.)
> 2. Do not encroach on other persons or their property. (Maybury explains that this is the basis for tort, or criminal, law.)

This system of law was sometimes referred to as *natural law*, because its two tenets represent inalienable rights, such as the right to life and freedom, granted not by a government but by a Higher Authority. This collection of precedents came to be called *case law*, and eventually became known as Common Law.

Maybury believes that Common Law, as expressed in the two laws above, is essential for the establishment and survival of an advanced society. The first law gives rise to trade, specialization, and contract. The second law creates peace, security, and goodwill. Maybury further suggests that the closer any government can come to honoring these two laws, the more successful it will be, whereas the more a government loses sight of these laws, the more their liberty and prosperity will decline.

The feudal governments of the Dark Ages hated these Common Laws, and did not feel they were under any obligation to obey them. The judges found themselves caught in the middle, under a great deal of pressure to accommodate the brutal territorial lords. The feudal lords asserted their power by declaring that they had the divine right of kings, that they were descended from the deities. Thus they placed themselves above the Common Law.

Thanks to their divine right, the kings were able to keep the serfs in poverty, to which the secret orders had become immune by means of their large underground economy. With the advent of shipbuilding technology, more and more people began to escape this oppression by going to America. They took this underground economy there with them, where it continued to flourish. Almost everyone in the new land was engaged in smuggling or tax evasion.

Conditions were harsh on board the ships bound for the New World. Children under seven years of age seldom survived. Dysentery, scurvy, typhus and other diseases killed off many adults during the long journey over rough seas. When the Pilgrims arrived on the Mayflower, they did what the earlier arrivals had done: they established a system of socialism, though it was not called that at the time. All profit gained by any means, including fishing, farming, working, trade, or traffic, was placed in the common stock of the colony. In turn, all persons of the community were fed from this common stock.

William Bradford, the governor of Plymouth, reported that the colonists who landed in 1621 went hungry for the first couple of years because they preferred to steal rather than work in the fields. The same thing had happened in Jamestown in 1607, where half the settlers had died in the first year. The first Thanksgiving was not so much a celebration as it was a last meal for those who would die during the winter.

In 1623 Bradford replaced the socialistic order with a free market system, in which he gave each household a parcel of land and told them they could keep whatever they produced or trade it away as they saw fit. The harvest in 1623 was much more robust than in the previous two years, and no one went hungry. In fact, the farmers produced so much food that by 1624 they started exporting corn. Before there were free markets, there had been nothing to be thankful for.

One tradition that did carry over to the New World was contempt for the English government and its attempts to tax the people. America was a huge underground economy based on free trade and enterprise, inhabited by rebellious, individualistic smugglers and tax evaders. But by the 1760s America had become one of the most prosperous places on earth, and the English government began to impose more taxes on the colonies to support the British Empire. Britain's attempt to put a halt to smuggling in the American colonies was the primary cause of the Revolutionary War.

However, the colonists were strongly committed to the Common Law. In fact, in his book *Law In America*, Bernard Schwartz tells us that Thomas Gage, the British Governor of Massachusetts in 1774, complained that Americans were hard to buffalo because so many of them were lawyers! The colonists were adamant about their study and understanding of the law, as it was the basis on which they were able to plan for the future of their work, their trade, and their investments.

It is interesting to note that being a member of a secret society, such as the Masons, carried with it at the time much more than simply an opportunity to participate in an underground organization. Success in the legal profession was almost a prerequisite for holding governmental office. The sons of the wealthy, who could afford to study at the Temple in London, were assured access to public office if they so desired, for the Temple was a bastion of the Templar stronghold. In fact, the term "passing the bar" originated with the Knights Templar, according to Sora, and still stands today as a rite of passage that must be achieved before one can practice law. Needless to say, the secret and elite structures that have built America's business empires and family fortunes have done a great job of concealing their disreputable past. We will look into this subject in future chapters.

The foundation for the American Revolution was established by Reverend John Mayhew in a sermon on January 30, 1750, which was read by almost all of the colonists. Mayhew argued that there is a law higher than any governmental law, and that the people are only required to obey their government's law when it is in alignment with this Higher Law. It was this Higher Law that was the basis for the Common Law that governed the lives of the colonists. This was the law the colonists were dedicated to, and they believed that the politicians and the government of England were encroaching on their freedoms.

In the Declaration of Independence, the colonists stated that they were disbanding the bonds that had connected them to England so that they could assume the rights entitled them by "the Laws of Nature and Nature's God."

The Founding Fathers were well read. One would have to assume they had at least a passing knowledge of the Bible, the Torah, and the Koran, and were familiar with the names of Jesus, Abraham, and

Mohammad. Certainly they were aware that no one had ever produced a document that could be verified as having been written by God. And yet they referred to "the Laws of Nature and Nature's God."

It is obvious that our Founding Fathers believed in God, yet they did not refer to any specific religion or savior. This is extremely important, for it would have been so easy for them to refer to the Christian tradition in some way. Instead, it was "the Laws of Nature and Nature's God" they spoke of, careful not to show any religious preference. I cannot put words into the mouths of our Founding Fathers, but it seems obvious that they spoke of God in this universal way for a reason. Could it be that they wanted to allow this new government to be based on the broadest and most common understanding of the Creator?

I believe this was exactly the case. They were aware of how divisive the teachings of religion could be; they were all familiar with the many trials and tribulations wrought upon Europe in the name of religion. Therefore, when they detailed the inalienable rights of life, liberty, and the pursuit of happiness, they refused to specify any particular religion. I believe this might be the single most overlooked aspect of the United States Constitution. This is of no small import, for the Constitution is one of the most important documents of all time. No other set of ideas or principles was ever so pivotal in the founding of a nation.

Different religions speak of God in different ways. It has been said that more wars have been fought over religion than for any other reason. Even today, with radical terrorist groups calling for a Holy War against America, religion cannot be dismissed. The issue of God has become so controversial that the Supreme Court has gotten involved, and the nation is being fractured over the idea of a Supreme Being.

Therefore, it is essential that our understanding of God include a broader perspective, something that is inclusive rather than exclusive. Our forefathers wanted a system of government that answered to a Higher Authority. They wanted a government based on the Laws of Nature, laws that echoed the very voice of God. It would have been so easy for them to speak of the Bible, or of Jesus. But these were men who paid attention to detail. Instead, they went to great lengths to resist defining their idea of God as the traditional Christian concept of European culture.

Looking to the precision of the Founding Fathers' words, I believe they had in mind something other than using the credo of Christianity as the basis upon which the Republic would stand. In fact, there is a group on the Internet that claims that the Bible was not the basis on which the Constitution was formed, and for this reason they are claiming that the Constitution broke the preexisting colonial covenant with God. This site can be found at www.ismellarat.com. They quote Patrick Henry: "Here is a revolution as radical as that which separated us from Great Britain." Patrick Henry refused his invitation to attend the Constitutional Convention in 1787 for just this reason—that the Constitution was not, in fact, Bible-based.

In order to promote the ideals of liberty and to curb the potential for politicians to abuse the power of their office, our forefathers wanted as small and as powerless a government as possible. Thomas Paine expressed this sentiment when he said in his book, *Common Sense*, that even in its best state, government is nothing but a necessary evil. Our Founding Fathers were adamant about founding a Republic, for they knew that the most enlightened government was one that governed with a very light touch. Therefore, it was to the Republic that they were conceding authority, and the democratic principles seemed the best means by which to insure the survival of the Republic. To protect the individual liberties of the people, as soon as the Constitution was completed they immediately wrote the Bill of Rights, based on the precepts of Common Law.

The founding of America meant for the first time that a system of government was in place to protect the average person who did not have access to wealth from family breeding and connection. Once ordinary individuals were given the basic protections accorded by a divine Creator, they were free to use their individual talents and abilities to accumulate wealth, position, and power. This was unheard of in Western civilization prior to this time.

This basic concept has altered our world more than any single event in history. It did not and could not guarantee that all individuals would always have equal opportunity. There never has been, nor will there ever be, a system that can determine how much determination, inspiration, or perspiration it will take to succeed in any given industry or occupation.

There will always be some who are favored by genetics, luck, or family ties. The American Dream was born of the fact that no one can legislate a level playing field. No government will ever be able to replace God, because human beings always have been and will continue to be fallible creatures. There is no way to legislate success, because only the human spirit is capable of reaching for the stars.

The American Revolution began in the hearts and minds of our forefathers, and they invested an enormous amount of thought to give us what they believed were the best tools for success. Their work has produced a highly advanced and prosperous nation based on the belief that there is a Higher Authority to which we all answer. Now it is up to us to find the common ground, for if we cannot find a way to use it to bring us together, there are those who would use it to tear us apart.

3

A HOUSE DIVIDED AGAINST ITSELF

The history of the Catholic Church has been very much shrouded in secrecy from the beginning. It is reputed to be one of the wealthiest organizations in the world, with untold treasures and fortunes hidden safe in the tombs of the Vatican. Being the one true voice of God since the time of Rome and throughout the Dark Ages afforded it a head start in its pursuit of material wealth.

In his book *A Woman Rides the Beast*, Dave Hunt points out that the Roman Catholic Church has never admitted any wrongdoing in regard to the Inquisition, murdering thousands of Jews, slaughtering one million Serbs during World War II, or smuggling tens of thousands of Nazi war criminals to safety.

According to Hunt, the Catholic Church has revised the Bible and its codes of conduct to suit its own needs. He points out that the reason celibacy was instituted into the organization had nothing to do with the purity that comes from dedicating oneself to God, but rather stemmed from the fact that the pope didn't want the priests to have any heirs who might lay claim to the riches of the church.

Over the last few centuries the common man has survived and prospered under a free enterprise system that guarantees basic human rights. And the Catholic Church has managed to survive, whereas the concept of royalty has all but died out, with a few minor exceptions that usually exist in title only. The secret societies have also survived, but only because they have been able to remain almost invisible, silently pulling the strings in the background while others struggle to understand what is happening in our fast-paced society.

As we saw in the 2004 election, the politics of religion played an important part in the final decision. It seems that for the last 20 years there has been an increasingly strong drive on the part of some to eliminate any reference to God when it comes to the function of government or anything related to government funding. The voices of protest on both sides have become rather strident. But how do we account for this when atheists account for a very small percentage of the population?

Certainly, a portion of the drive to remove all reference to God from government is that, as pointed out in the previous chapter, many people don't want one denomination to be promoted to the exclusion of others. Another reason is that there have been many instances of parental violence and abuse in the name of the Lord. In these situations a parent might claim to be punishing a child so that he or she would be worthy of heaven and not suffer eternal damnation. But this is a sorry excuse for preaching religious doctrine, and invariably has more to do with the pathology of the parent than with the problem of the child.

And of course everyone is familiar with the recent discoveries of abuse within the priesthood. But these are the exceptions rather than the rule, and although this doesn't excuse the behavior, it seems silly to condemn an entire religion because of a few degenerates. However, it is my sense that there is more to the recent upswing against religion, and we will take another look at this issue in chapter 21.

Abraham Lincoln once said something to the effect that he prayed not for God to be on our side, but for us to be on God's side. This is an incredibly profound and elegant concept of truth. There are those who might suggest that the worlds of spirituality and politics are incompatible, the strangest of bedfellows. But there has to be a thread of connectivity, some standard of measure that recognizes truth, honesty, and responsibility in politics.

Many of our Presidents have had a strong belief in God, and prayed often. John Kennedy, the first Catholic President, was very open about his Catholicism. He was also clear that whatever his personal beliefs, he would not foist them upon the nation, that he and he alone would be responsible for his decisions. He accepted his responsibility, acknowledging that if he made a mistake the blame would fall on his shoulders and not on God.

I think John Kennedy was saying that the highest truth comes from within, from one's individual relationship with God. He knew that he wouldn't be able to offer any quotes of wisdom from the Bible to justify his decisions, but he trusted in his relationship with the Almighty. He didn't hold that his God was bigger than my God or your God, just that he would do his best to listen to the guidance of the Holy Spirit. He was following in Lincoln's footsteps, and that seems to me a worthwhile pursuit.

This is important, because President Bush has stated that God is a constant source of influence in his life and his decisions as President. He has gone so far as to imply that with God on his side it is impossible for him to make mistakes, and this is where he steps in the deep stuff. To suggest that America should go to war because God has ordained this country to spread freedom and democracy to the rest of the world is blasphemy. How can he possibly claim that his God is more knowing and wiser than anyone else's God, whether Hindu, Jewish, or Muslim?

It was a successful tactic as far as winning an election goes, but is Bush right to take such an arrogant position? Whether we believe in God or not, shouldn't we all try to honor Maybury's second rule and not encroach on other persons or their property? If we encroach on another's belief system, aren't we encroaching on them? Until God comes down to earth and shows Himself, we should honor everyone's right to worship God in whatever manner they choose, so long as they afford us the same right.

As I write this book there are many schisms that divide America, that are causing unbelievable discord. We have too many serious and threatening problems facing us to fight over whose God is bigger. Unless we can find common ground and eliminate the needless fights and arguments, we will not be able to solve the challenging issues facing us. The overriding bond that unites us is the spirit of liberty and individualism. These two towers of freedom will always stand taller than the highest skyscraper. They have allowed us to build the American Dream.

4

A TALE OF TWO PARTIES

America was shocked by the events of September 11. Like Abraham Lincoln, we wanted to believe that there was no giant that could step across the Atlantic Ocean and invade us. Our invasion of Afghanistan was an obvious first move to disrupt the hornet's nest. But President Bush ignored what should have been the obvious second step: to secure our borders and to finally begin enforcing our immigration laws. Having secure borders is the nation's first line of defense against terrorism. Instead he began a campaign intended to excite our worst fear: that Iraq had weapons of mass destruction.

As the facts finally came out, Bush's popularity at the polls declined. His failure to win the peace has caused more people to doubt the wisdom of his decision to invade Iraq. But I still could not understand his refusal to enforce the law by securing our borders. So I decided to so some research on my own. The things I discovered revealed a level of deceit so pervasive that I was shocked. I had not been prepared to discover that our government is being destroyed from within. These discoveries have prompted me to write this book.

There can be no doubt that we are under attack by radical Muslim terrorists, and this book is in large part an attempt to explain the roots of this war. But we have to admit the facts before we can determine a course of action. In his book *Imperial Hubris*, Michael Scheuer states that terrorism and guerrilla warfare are not the cause of this war, but only its symptoms. When a war is being waged against a superior power, one uses whatever tools are available. Terrorism is the poor man's way of waging war. Scheuer, also known as Anonymous, worked in the CIA for 17 years as a specialist in the Middle East. He left the CIA and has revealed his identity because he believes the U.S. has failed to comprehend some crucial elements of this crisis, and that we are seriously underestimating our enemy.

Looking back to our beginnings as a nation, the first duty of our government was to protect the life, liberty, and property of the citizens of the United States. But our Founding Fathers did not trust human nature, and they wanted to make it difficult for a single individual to embroil us in a war. So they set up a government that included a system of checks and balances.

James Madison warned that the accumulation of power in one branch of government was the very definition of tyranny. He also said, "War is, in fact, the true source of executive aggrandizement." Therefore, Congress was given the power to declare war, while the President was to oversee its execution

Thomas Jefferson warned us to avoid the mutual jealousies and complicated alliances of the Europeans, that we never take an active part in their quarrels, calling them "nations of eternal war." America heeded this advice until just before the turn of the twentieth century.

By the 1890s, America was the industrial leader of the world, and our government watched as European leaders continued to expand their empires. Teddy Roosevelt had agitated for America to expand its influence in the world, and President McKinley saw an opportunity to do just that as Cuba continued its struggle for freedom from Spain. He ordered the battleship Maine into Havana Harbor. When the Maine blew up mysteriously, it was blamed on the Spanish, and Congress declared war on Spain, the weakest of the European powers. We took Cuba and the Philippines as our prize.

While the Cubans accepted their fate and were allowed a small form of self-government, this was not the case with the Philippines, a group of 7,000 islands 5,000 miles from America. The Filipinos wanted their independence and started a guerrilla war against the U.S. They knew the land, so they could strike and then easily disappear. Guerrilla warfare is the most difficult, most frustrating type of war to fight, as we would later find out in Vietnam.

Frustrated, General Smith told his troops, "I want no prisoners. I wish you to burn and kill; the more you burn and kill, the better it will please me" (this according to John Bowman's *Almanac Of America's Wars*). This was the beginning of America's quest for an empire under the heading of Manifest Destiny. 220,000 Filipino men, women, and children were killed, and the policy of using American soldiers for purposes other than national defense was solidified. The Maine was raised and examined in 1911, and in 1970 Admiral Rickover declared that the coalbunker explosion had been spontaneous, a common occurrence in that era.

In 1916 Woodrow Wilson campaigned for reelection saying he would keep us out of the war, and shortly after his election we were fighting in World War I. Wilson was the first to speak of *making the world safe for democracy*, and he won the political elite of this country over to the idea of global intervention. Henry Luce, through his publishing empire (Time, Life, and Fortune) was avid in his push to enter the war. Luce envisioned a twentieth century of power and glory for America.

During the 1930s Hollywood turned out numerous films glamorizing everything English, and even promoting Stalin's Russia in films like *North Star* and *Mission to Moscow*. With all these anti-Nazi films, not a single film was made depicting the millions of people Stalin was murdering at the very same time.

But it was Harry Truman who began the frontal assault on the Constitutional dictates of the United States. In his essay "The Case for an America First Foreign Policy," published in Richard Ebeling and Jacob Hornberger's anthology *The Failure of America's Foreign Wars*, Ralph Raico notes that Truman did not even ask Congress for a declaration of war. Instead, Truman used the U.N. Security Council's condemnation of North Korea as his authority. Raico states that Truman had even hoped Russia would veto the U.N. condemnation and thus make it crystal-clear that he, as President, had the power to plunge the nation into war on his own authority.

In his farewell address to the nation, President Eisenhower made it clear that we have to be concerned about the rise of an immense military establishment and a large arms industry, and that we must guard against their undue influence. He warned that the more influence wielded by the military/industrial complex, the more likely we would be the victims of its disastrous misplaced power.

Before the 1964 election, Lyndon Johnson said we would not send our boys 10,000 miles away from home to do what the Asians should be doing for themselves. But by August of '64 he was supporting South Vietnamese commando attacks in North Vietnam, for which he had no authority, and he then proceeded to distort the facts before Congress with the Gulf of Tonkin Resolution. By providing false documentation he received his authorization to use armed force, and more than 58,000 American soldiers died.

The first President Bush began sending troops to Saudi Arabia for the Gulf War without Congressional approval, relying instead on U.N. authorization. A year later he would state that he didn't need permission from some old goat in Congress to kick Saddam out of Kuwait.

Bill Clinton moved up by 24 hours his planned invasion of Haiti to avoid a negative Congressional vote, but did press the United Nations for its blessings, according to Doug Bandow in his essay "The Power to Declare War," also published in *The Failure of America's Foreign Wars*. Clinton also took action in Korea, Bosnia, and Somalia without engaging Congress in the decision-making process. In 1993 he even stated, "I would strenuously oppose attempts to encroach on the President's foreign policy powers."

During the 2000 election campaign, George Bush criticized the Clinton foreign policy's emphasis on nation building, claiming that he would bring greater humility to American foreign policy. Yet his attempt to democratize terrorism out of existence in Iraq is nation building to the extreme.

As a general rule, Americans have very little interest in foreign policies. We are much more interested in reaching financial goals, saving for college educations, and raising our families than we are about the problems and histories of foreign countries. So while we are busy with our lives, special interest groups lobby the politicians to support their export trade and foreign investments. This allows them to use the Department of Defense, the Navy, the Marines, and whatever other means prove necessary to protect their private interests, at the taxpayers' expense.

Both parties have learned that when a President "gets tough" with some evil foreign ruler, he gets a "shot in the arm" in the polls. For this reason, foreign interventions have often been more a matter of party politics than of the well being of America. The politicians have learned the art of creating a warlike sense of hysteria to further their political agendas. The 50-year Cold War with the Soviet Union promoted one episode of hysteria after another, with no formal declaration of war by Congress. These included soldiers dying in Korea and Vietnam, foreign governments being overthrown and dictators installed, secret wars being waged in Cambodia and Laos, and "covert operations" that were carried out in a host of other countries.

It is clear that our leaders tend to encroach on the rights and property of other nations, as Maybury would put it, to bolster their own lagging popularity. Truman established a dangerous precedent by not seeking Congressional authorization before going to war. Congress should be made party to such decisions before the body bags are counted.

The bottom line is that when it comes to foreign policy, the trend has been for U.S. Presidents of both parties to expand their power base by getting involved in foreign disputes. Then the government shamelessly prints money to finance their power grabs, fueling the fires of inflation, while taxes are usually raised and the debt grows larger. Meanwhile, the real problems of the nation go unaddressed. Our freedoms are diminished, poverty, drugs, and welfare are perpetuated, new political favorites are established, and the American Dream grows dimmer.

The essence of our government should be to protect us from those who would commit crimes such as murder, rape, and robbery, to prosecute and convict such criminals, and to defend our borders against invasion. The history of liberty is the history of limiting governmental power. However, for more than a century, our government has used foreign policy to expand its authority and to continually diminish our freedoms.

Our Founding Fathers gave us the best system of government ever devised and told us what to do: stay strong enough to defend ourselves, conduct trade with all partners, and stay out of political entanglements. They promoted neutrality, not isolationism. We used to be able to trade with other countries, regardless of their politics, so long as they treated us fairly. Now our politicians try to scare the hell out of us whenever they need a political boost.

Ralph Raico says this constant state of national emergency cost us $10 trillion between 1948 and 1989, based on 1993 dollars. Citing Dr.

Robert Higgs as his source, Raico says this does not include the costs of veterans' benefits or foreign aid. Again, the warning of James Madison's looms large, that the executive department is most distinguished by the propensity to war. Spoken so long ago, his words carry more weight today than ever.

Thus it has become increasingly difficult to differentiate between political parties when it comes to war. Both parties share a philosophy that gives them the right to involve the American people in any conflict of their choosing. They send our children off to die so that some multinational corporation can give an uplifting address at its annual shareholders meeting. They have corrupted our way of life, and it is time for them to stand accountable. The two-party system is dead in all but name, as both parties are willing to make a deal with the devil for the right price.

5

A NATION OF ADDICTS

The rhetoric of the 2004 election was filled with hate and hyperbole. Both parties played to the lowest common denominator, intent on agitating their followers into an angry mob mentality. The spin-doctors and the candidates deftly ignored any and all sensitive political issues. Election rage escalated as November approached; a fistfight erupted on one college campus because two students failed to agree on which candidate Jesus would vote for. Things were going from the ridiculous to the insane.

It was guerrilla warfare, and the rules of engagement instructed new party recruits on how to preach the party line to the unwashed masses. In his book *If It's Not Close They Can't Cheat*, Hugh Hewitt advised neophytes to avoid issues that were at all divisive and never to criticize a member of their own party, no matter how wrong they might be. In his book *Had Enough? A Handbook for Fighting Back*, James Carville counseled volunteers to keep their message simple, because the election would turn on the votes of illiterate people. Above all, both parties were committed to the ideology of winning at any cost.

Today, we as a nation are conveniently divided into two groups, liberals on the Left and conservatives on the Right. The liberals believe in social freedoms and the ability of the government to engineer a better world. They tend to believe in taxation as a means to control production and redistribute wealth. The conservatives are somewhat opposite, in that they believe trade and production should be unregulated, taxes low, and moral values legislated. Although these are rather general descriptions, they do provide a limited framework for understanding what each party will do when it gets into power. However, what a politician promises to do when they get elected and what they actually do are often quite different.

Our Founding Fathers believed that power is a corrupting influence, and that the longer a person is in a position of power, the more corrupt he becomes. They believed in keeping the government weak and small, so that people with good intentions wouldn't get carried away with the overwhelming intoxication afforded by their position.

There can be no doubt that today the large majority of our politicians are quite addicted to the power of their office. As a ruling body, our politicians are among the most powerful group of leaders in the world, yet they have become more deceitful than ever. For many of them, their only goal now appears to be getting reelected. And they have discovered that the best way to get reelected is to vote for ever larger "entitlements."

FDR was the first to employ this idea of entitlements in a major way. Knowing that people were embarrassed by the idea of accepting handouts, he invented ways to disguise them. Social Security taxes were called "contributions," making it sound as if it were some kind of insurance contract with the government. In the December 6, 2004 issue of *The American Conservative*, James Payne estimates that the overhead cost of Social Security comes to approximately one hundred percent of the benefits, due to government bureaucracy.

Here is a definition of *bureaucracy,* according to WEBSTERS II New Riverside University Dictionary: 2. Government marked by diffusion of authority among numerous offices and adherence to inflexible rules of operation. 3. An administrative system in which the need to follow complex procedures impedes effective action.

The pork barrel spending of our politicians is absurd. But our government's bureaucratic waste is equally staggering. The destruction of capital, which could be used productively to solve our problems, is enormous. Yet with each passing decade those in Washington become more corrupt. The large majority of our politicians have become nothing more than political whores, willing to say anything to get elected. During the last election one Senator proclaimed that all Americans should be entitled to a good health care program without having to go bankrupt. This made for a sweet campaign slogan, but it stands in stark contrast to the fact that this nation is fast approaching bankruptcy and may have to cut benefits.

Senator Hollings, who decided to retire instead of running for reelection in 2004, explained why. He said it was no longer about serving the public, but all about raising money to get reelected. He estimated that to be competitive he had to raise $30,000 each and every week. He said senators don't go to the Senate floor anymore, as they are too busy working the phones, and that they no longer work on Fridays because they have to go home and attend fund-raising events. Senators no longer even write their own legislation. Instead, special interest groups now write the legislation and give it to their Senator for review. How many of these bills favor the special interest group that does the writing? I wonder.

We, the American people, have come to believe that the government should take care of our every need, wipe away every tear. In effect, the politicians have created a society of addicts just like themselves, and our relationship is that of pusher/user. We press our leaders for ever-greater entitlements, and they keep trying to oblige so that they can get their drug of choice: POLITICAL POWER. The politicians have created a parasitic system of addiction that keeps a large portion of society sucking at the government's teat.

What if you and I paid our bills each month by using a credit card? And when the credit card bill came due we simply applied for another one? What if we continued to do this every few months? It wouldn't take long for the banks to cut off our credit. But there is no one cutting off the credit of the U.S. government. In fact, it would appear that the Federal Reserve has a vested interest in extending our debt even further (we will look at this again in chapters 10 and 11).

The control of our debt problems may soon be out of our hands. If other countries begin demanding higher and higher interest rates as our debt becomes ever more risky, the interest alone could choke us to death—which is just what is happening to our government. George Bush ran for office as a fiscal conservative in 2000, and yet he did not veto a single bill in his first four years, and the budget deficit exploded at a ferocious pace. Vice-President Cheney almost dismissed the budget deficit entirely when he said it was nothing more than numbers on paper. And his budget for fiscal year 2004-2005 included more than $16 billion of pork barrel spending.

Doug Bandow points out in *The American Conservative*, December 6, 2004 that Bush actually engineered one of the largest expansions of the welfare state in decades. In an effort to beat the Democrats to the punch for the senior citizen vote, he supported an extremely expensive prescription drug bill, and then lied about its cost to push it through Congress. The only complaint the liberals registered was that the bill should have been bigger, more expensive.

Bush has been employing the "fig leaf of empowerment" philosophy, which has much in common with FDR's approach. Bandow explains that this was how he sold his faith-based initiative allowing religious social services to compete with secular organizations for federal grants. As if that weren't bad enough, he then used it as a campaign tool to lobby grant recipients for their support in the 2004 election. He completely ignored the conservative position that a small government is best, substituting a more Left-leaning philosophy that a bigger government is the solution to America's problems.

At the Democratic Convention, Barack Obama asked this rhetorical question: "Are we not our brother's keeper?" He was greeted with wild applause. When I was in school he would have been labeled a Marxist, a Communist. Now he is regarded as a savior, a strong pair of shoulders upon which the Democrats are building their future. And it is this unspoken conspiracy between our dealer/politicians and the voter/ addicts that is heading us toward the status of a third-world country.

Jesse Jackson spoke of welfare in moral terms when Anderson Cooper interviewed him in October, 2004, on CNN. He asked, "When I am hungry, should you not feed me? When I am naked, should you not clothe me?" Has he forgotten the moral of teaching someone to fish so that they can become a responsible citizen rather than an addict?

In the 2004 election we saw the depth both parties will stoop to for political power. Each half-truth and lie was promoted in simple sound bites as they competed to serve the American people. But our well-being was not their main concern. Both Presidential candidates made promises of hope and optimism that were way out of touch with reality. How can we increase government benefits when we cannot meet our current obligations, except with more debt? This is the behavior of addicts!

Even in our domestic policy, it has become increasingly difficult to predict what our Presidents will do, as opposed to what they promise when they are trying to get elected. Both parties share a similar philosophy: that the people and their institutions can be perfected, if we can but find the right combination of spending, regulations, and war. Both parties, it seems, are willing to sell their soul to get reelected.

Certainly it is necessary that we take care of the sick, the poor, and the elderly. But it is also imperative that we stop the process of enabling. Trying to provide a panacea for every human failure is not the answer. Like a drug, welfare robs the individual of the resolve to exercise their talents to find creative solutions to their problems.

We need to begin to see that the obstacles life presents us are really opportunities to develop our strength and courage. Our hardships and failures are like the cocoon the butterfly struggles against to be free. Without the struggle, the wings would not grow strong, and the butterfly might not fly. It is the effort that builds the wings. Without the struggle, our wings do not grow strong, and our ability to soar, to solve our problems, is diminished.

Likewise, it is essential that those on the Right realize that it is impossible to legislate morality. Simply putting laws on the books does not change the way a person feels. It is essential that we have laws that protect our children from pedophiles and those who would prey on children. But we will never be able to pass a law that will change what is in a person's mind or heart. We can only pass strong laws that will hopefully act as a deterrent against criminal behavior, and then we must strenuously enforce those laws.

Most of our politicians are too addicted to the power and perks of their office to have the strength or courage to change their ways. But we, the people, must—unless we are willing to let the American Dream perish. Our free lunch system of government is degrading the spirit of America. Certainly there is more that we as a nation can do to improve our education, to eliminate waste, and to strengthen our liberties. But when our cries of self-pity and victimization drown out all other sounds, we can be certain the death knell is sounding.

6

THE DOGS OF WAR

Over the course of history it has been estimated that there have been more than 14,000 wars, and that they have resulted in 3.6 billion deaths. So states James Dunnigan in his book, *Dirty Little Secrets*. The two-hundred-year Pax Romana was actually anything but peaceful. It was filled with tyranny and terror, foreign wars and civil wars, rebellions and assassinations.

Our Founding Fathers knew the consequences of war, and warned us to forego political alliances with other countries. They believed political power corrupts the morals and judgment of our leaders, and therefore they wanted a small and weak central government.

They preached neutrality. Both James Madison and Alexander Hamilton spoke of the Swiss government in The Federalist Papers. Most Americans are ignorant of how Switzerland, a tiny country surrounded by warring nations, was able to stay out of two world wars. It is an interesting story. The Swiss government requires that all men join the militia at age 20 and become proficient marksmen trained to kill the officers of any invading army. They train regularly until they are 50. The officers on both sides in World War I and World War II were well aware of this fact, and were afraid to enter Switzerland, for they knew they would have targets on their chest. In both wars they convinced their superiors not to invade.

In 1870 the French lost the Franco-Prussian War, a bitter defeat because it saw the Prussians enter the city of Paris. Germany first became a nation in 1871, after this war. Speaking the same language, Germany joined with the Austro-Hungarian Empire, long an enemy of the French Empire. The Russians, who had been competing with the Austro-Hungarians for land and taxpayers for some time, joined with the French Empire to form an alliance. The Italians didn't like the French, so they joined with the Austro-Hungarian Empire. And the British Empire, worried about the military buildup in Germany, allied with the French. Then the Serbs and Russians, both Orthodox Christian, formed an alliance against the Turks, who were Muslim.

By 1914, Europe had divided into two large gangs furiously building armies and training troops. Over the past several thousand years these groups had fought each other many times, often over who would get to claim a particular territory.

On June 28, 1914, a Serb in Bosnia killed the heir to the Austro-Hungarian throne, and the dogs of war were released. The two European gangs renewed their drama of eternal warfare. But by the spring of 1917, half of the French combat divisions had refused further orders to attack, Russian units were in revolt against their government, and a peace movement had developed in Austria. According to John Keegan's *A History Of Warfare*, there was widespread feeling that the war was falling apart, that it would just grind to a halt. On Christmas in 1914 and 1915, troops from both sides left their trenches to sing carols and play soccer with the men they had been fighting the day before.

When the war erupted, President Wilson declared that the U.S. would remain neutral, yet he struck a secret deal with Britain to sell them weapons and supplies. The German Embassy in Washington D.C. had publicly warned Americans not to travel on the Lusitania before it set sail for England. In fact, their Embassy had taken out ads in 50 newspapers, most of them on the Eastern seaboard, warning Americans not to sail on the Lusitania. The Lusitania actually set sail with many famous passengers on board and 5,500 cases of ammunition, which was kept secret from all of the passengers. The Lusitania was torpedoed on May 7, 1915, and 124 Americans lost their lives. President Wilson then committed the American Navy to protecting these arms shipments. In 1916 Wilson campaigned with the slogan that he would keep the United States out of the war. One month later he proclaimed that we had to enter the war *to make the world safe for democracy*, and now the European conflict became the Great War. Instead of choosing neutrality, Wilson joined with the Allies, and the European stalemate was ended.

The U.S. government waged an all-out propaganda campaign painting all Germans as bloodthirsty, satanic monsters who wanted to rule the world. Anyone who wanted to stay out of the war was called an isolationist. The French, the British, and the Russians had spent centuries building their empires, and had already attacked and conquered about a third of the world. But as Ronald Schaffer tells us in his book, *America in the Great War*, it was the German soldiers who were depicted in lurid posters as wild-eyed monsters intent on world domination and destroying the skyscrapers of New York.

By 1918 the Germans were crushed, and the Treaty of Versailles forced reparations on Germany that stripped them of 132 million gold marks, much of their natural mineral deposits, and all overseas financial assets. The port of Danzig was taken from them, as well as West Prussia and Posen. Their navy was abolished, and Germany was forbidden to keep an army, among other things. In effect, the French were punishing the Germans for their defeat in the Franco-Prussian war nearly 50 years earlier.

The Treaty of Versailles was actually the beginning of World War II. The British blockade of Germany after the war caused the starvation of 800,000 Germans. The only way the Germans could pay off their debt was to print more money, which caused the hyperinflation of the 1920s. By 1924, millions of Germans who had been middle class or rich now wondered where their next meal was coming from. The poverty and anger of the German people left them ripe for Hitler's propaganda.

The U.S. Federal Reserve tried to help them out with loans, and began to expand the U.S. money supply. Between 1924 and 1930, it was American investors who lent Germany most of the seven billion dollars they borrowed. Much of the newly created money from the Federal Reserve went into the stock market, creating a speculative bubble. In 1929 the Federal Reserve stopped its inflation of the money supply, causing the stock market to crash. What followed was The Great Depression, which spread throughout much of the world and sent Germany even deeper into poverty.

In order to understand President Wilson's change of heart about entering the European conflict, it might be worthwhile to examine some developments that occurred prior to the outbreak of war. Sometime during the latter part of the 19th century, a man named Cecil Rhodes and Lord Rothschild formed a secret organization known as the Milners Round Table, according to Anthony Sutton's book *America's Secret Establishment*. Rhodes, who had a strong desire to form a one-world government, was influential in helping to establish a group of semi-secret organizations that would become known as The Round Table Group and would eventually be known simply as the Group, headquartered at Oxford University.

Rhodes, whose DeBeers Company owned 91% of the world's diamond mines in 1891, became a very wealthy man. At his death in 1902 his entire fortune was left to Oxford University, which then began the famous Rhodes Scholarship fund. Oxford University is well known for supporting the idea of a one-world government. The Group was thus able to become a very formidable influence on world affairs and politics, though always behind the scenes. It is at this time that we see a number of tax-exempt organizations begin to spring up in the United States with the idea of world peace central to their philosophy.

In his exposé, *The Tax-Exempt Foundations*, William H. McIlhany reveals the minutes from one of these "peace "organizations that was actually compiled several years before the outbreak of World War I. This organization was the Carnegie Endowment for International Peace, and the trustees were trying to determine how to best alter the character of American society, that it might become a socialistic state. The decision was reached that war was the most effective way to alter the life of an entire people, making them more receptive to socialism. The question was then raised, how do we involve the U.S. in a war? Their conclusion was that by infiltrating the U.S. State Department they could help to shape American foreign policy and influence war making decisions.

In a meeting around May 1917 these trustees congratulated themselves on the wisdom of their original decision, for the war had indeed impacted life in the U.S. They even had the audacity to send President Wilson a telegram telling him not to end the war too quickly. Now it was their goal to see that life in the U.S. did not revert to the limited scope prior to 1914. To do this they knew that education was the key. They then approached the Rockefeller Foundation and asked them to take on the task of controlling the educational system that related to domestic issues. The Carnegie trustees would handle the issues that involved international significance.

Many of the programs thought necessary for the formation of a one-world government were consolidated under the influence of the Council of Foreign Relations (CFR), which was established in 1921 in America. The European branch of this organization had already been established in Paris in 1919 and became known as the Royal Institute of International Affairs, and also as Chatham House. One of the first acts of the CFR was to establish periodicals such as *Foreign Affairs, Current History*, and *The American Journal of International Law*. Funded by tens of millions of dollars from foundations that were controlled by CFR members such as Carnegie, Rockefeller, and Twentieth Century, CFR took the lead in setting American policy on many issues that supported a one-world government.

The profound influence on American politics of the CFR and a group of adjunct organizations such as the Atlantic Council, Trilateral Commission, Bilderbergs, Aspen Institute, and Foreign Policy Association has been enormous. William F. Jasper points out in his book *Global Tyranny... Step-By-Step*, that American politics has been filled with members of these groups since the 1920's. Since 1921, 23 Secretaries of State have been members of the CFR, as well as 16 Secretaries of Defense (Rumsfeld asked that his name be taken off of their list), and 15 Directors of the CIA. The eight United States Presidents that were also members of the CFR are: Herbert Hoover, Dwight Eisenhower, Richard Nixon, Gerald Ford, Jimmy Carter, Bush Sr., Bill Clinton, and Bush Jr. (Kennedy supposedly asked that his name be removed). It might be fair to say that almost every American institution from the New York Times to the Daily Breeze in Southern California has been affected and influenced by the CFR, and still most Americans have never heard of this organization.

Colonel Edward Mandell House hosted the 1919 meeting in Paris that gave rise to the CFR. House was never in the military, but was given the title of Colonel by a governor of Texas, where House was a political "kingmaker." Thomas House, the Colonel's father, was a representative of the House of Rothschild during the Civil War, and the House family was one of the few Southern families that emerged after the war with a great deal of wealth. Colonel House personally selected Woodrow Wilson to run for the Presidency in 1912 and convinced the House of Morgan to back him.

House had been secretly plotting to get into the war in Europe soon after it started in 1914 while the House of Morgan was financing the debt of England and France, which soon reached $1.5 billion. By the war's end the House of Morgan had financed $9.5 billion of European debt. The reason so many Americans were on the Lusitania when it sunk was that the U.S. State Department had contacted all of the papers and convinced them to kill the ads placed by the German Embassy. The only newspaper that printed the ad was in Des Moines, Iowa. House knew that such a large casualty figure would certainly lead to America's entrance into the war.

President Wilson was so dependent on House that he referred to him as "my second personality," and said, "His thoughts and my thoughts are one." In his book *The Strangest Friendship in History: Woodrow Wilson and Colonel House*, George Sylvester Viereck describes Wilson's dependency on Colonel House as abnormal, and further states that to understand American political history in the ensuing decades it is essential to understand this relationship.

As early as the autumn of 1914 Wilson began talking about the necessity of a great association of nations. In May of 1916 Wilson spoke at the League to Enforce Peace banquet, where he advocated the idea with such vigor that he became regarded as the champion of the League of Nations. However, according to Viereck, it was House who wrote the first draft of the charter for the League of Nations. He also prevailed on Wilson to convene what became known as the "Inquiry," a cabal of Americans who favored a one-world government and formulated much of Wilson's Fourteen Points program for peace.

House authored a novel anonymously during the Presidential campaign of 1912 entitled *Philip Dru: Administrator*. House later admitted to authoring this novel in which the hero, Philip Dru, decries the travesty of American society in favor of Marxist socialism. Dru eventually becomes dictator of the United States and abolishes the Constitution to begin a Marxist government. In his novel House calls for a League of Nations–seven years before Wilson's formal proposal in Versailles. Some believe that House's novel is indispensable in understanding Wilson's New Freedom and Roosevelt's New Deal, for it outlines the shape of political evolution in America. Suffice it to say that the effect the CFR has had on American politics and history may just now be coming to light.

7

THE ROAD TO HELL IS PAVED WITH GOOD INTENTIONS

In 1918 Eleanor Roosevelt discovered that her husband had been having an affair with Lucy Mercer, her secretary. By this time FDR and Eleanor already had five children, and they agreed to stay together so as not to destroy FDR's political aspirations. (Indeed, it is my belief that it was FDR's strong political ambitions that prompted him to marry his cousin Eleanor, the niece of former President Theodore Roosevelt, in the first place.) In her book *No Ordinary Time*, Doris Kearns Goodwin maintains that FDR would later have several mistresses who lived with him quite openly in their mansion.

Eleanor's agreement to stay together was conditioned upon two demands: first, that she would no longer have to perform her "wifely duties," and second, that FDR would never again see Lucy. Their son Elliot has admitted that from that day on there was a great deal of tension whenever the family was together. Harry Truman once called FDR the coldest human being he had ever met. I mention this now because in a later chapter Bill Clinton will be faced with an altogether different choice when an affair of his is discovered.

The Great Depression was a watershed period in American history, for it saw our leaders abandon all semblance of the economic liberty that had made America an unparalleled success. Franklin Roosevelt was elected in 1932, and many consider him the greatest President of the twentieth century. In his book *FDR's Folly*, Jim Powell takes another look at FDR's impact on the depression. A member of the Cato Institute, Powell has done an incredible job of research and analysis on one of the most important periods in American history.

While not known for his intellectual prowess, FDR was a political genius. His fireside chats utilized the new medium of radio to influence the American people as never before. Almost overnight America watched as the parties and good times of the Roaring Twenties ground to a halt, replaced by long bread lines and soup kitchens. More than anything else, it was the persuasive voice of FDR that gave Americans a reason to hope.

The influence of the times was very much a factor in the policies of FDR as he attempted to remake the American economy. The Communist Revolution of 1917 attracted admirers in the U.S. As Powell points out, FDR believed the free enterprise system had created the Great Depression, and his policies were aimed at reform, not recovery.

When FDR took office, single-branch banks accounted for 90% of the banks in the country. They were poorly diversified because banking across state lines was prohibited. There had been 150 Congressional bills for federal deposit insurance, but the Senators with strong, well-diversified banks didn't want their banks to be penalized because other banks were less diversified.

After his inauguration, FDR issued Presidential Proclamation 2039, which closed the banks and resulted in the Glass-Steagall Act. FDR targeted the biggest banks in the country, because they were the only ones engaged in commercial banking as well as investment banking. Big was considered bad. It would have been far better if he had gotten rid of the unit banking laws and let the strong banks acquire the weaker branches. This would have solved the diversification problems and eliminated almost all of the risk of the small single-branch banks. It should be noted that during this time Canada did not have a single bank failure because it allowed banks to diversify. There were 10 banks with over 3,000 branches throughout the country, and no banking crisis!

Glass-Steagall authorized federal deposit insurance, but did not address the lack of trust in the system and did not end bank failures. All it did was delay the day of reckoning by not addressing the problem. The burden of the failures of the smaller, weaker banks was passed on to the taxpayers. The bill finally came due in the early 1980s when Bill Seidman was called in to deal with a banking crisis that amounted to hundreds of billions of dollars.

FDR was under pressure from the farmers who had elected him to do something about inflation. On March 6, 1933, he made it a crime for Americans to possess gold, and on March 10 he issued Executive Order (EO) 6037, which prohibited the removal of gold from the U.S. One of FDR's advisers, George Warren, was convinced that there was a correlation between gold and commodities, and he concluded that rising gold prices would cause higher farm prices. So on August 29, 1933, FDR issued EO 6261, which required all gold producers to sell their output to the Secretary of the Treasury, at prices determined by the Treasury.

Yet gold prices continued to rise while commodity prices and the dollar continued to fall, and in January, 1934, FDR decided to go back to pegging the dollar to gold. The dollar was now pegged at $35 per ounce of gold, up from the $20.67 that it had been at. And even though his gold buying scheme was a failure, the government kept all of the gold, worth seven billion dollars after the devaluation of the dollar.

The American people had already been hurt by the contracting dollar, yet FDR actually tripled taxes during the Great Depression, raising them from $1.6 billion in 1933 to $5.3 billion in 1940. The business community was quiet as he waged a moral crusade against free markets. Companies that retained 70% of their net income for investment were taxed at a rate of 73.91%. This was especially tough on small businesses because they had a more difficult time qualifying for loans.

Although the undistributed profits tax was repealed, there was still widespread fear of the federal government in the business community. FDR completely failed to bring about the adequate revival of private investment that could have led to higher employment. One of his own tax advisers, Randolph E. Paul, admitted that FDR's tax policies actually intensified the depression he claimed to have been trying to correct.

FDR condemned the capitalist despots, claiming that only the organized power of the government could help the American citizen. The Revenue Act of 1937 allowed Social Security taxes to be deducted from the payroll, which took more money out of the hands of the worker while state taxes were doubling between 1930 and 1940.

FDR's policy of giving the labor unions monopoly status also had a negative effect. His theory was that the depression was caused by falling wages, and that if the unions could force industries to pay above market minimum wages it would spell an end to the depression. Employers responded by increasing the mechanization of their industries, and were able to eliminate many unskilled workers. This fell most harshly on the poorest of all, the black workers.

Even the New York Times ran articles about irresponsible union bosses and their power, but FDR never made any effort to crack down on them. It was Robert Kennedy who finally tried to reign in the corrupt union bosses when he took Jimmy Hoffa and others like him to court in the early 1960s. But by then the power of the unions and their corruption was much greater, thanks to FDR. By January 1938, GM had dismissed a quarter of its employees, while other companies experienced similar job losses. The 1400 NRA officers in 54 state and branch offices tried to oversee every aspect of the production process. All thoughts of recovery were seemingly replaced by government control and reform as civil liberty violations and business failures continued to mount.

The monetary contraction of 1929-1933 hit America's six million farmers hard, partly because they had not recovered from the agricultural depression following World War I. The farmers had ramped up production during World War I to supply a hungry Europe, but even by 1929 there were still too many farmers and too many acres under cultivation. In May of 1933, the Agricultural Adjustment Act was passed to restrict farm production and purchase farm surpluses, but it did nothing to address the higher prices facing unemployed industrial workers.

Because the crop had already been planted when the agricultural bill was passed, the New Dealers decided they would have to destroy the current crop as it came to harvest. The effect was that men were destroying oats while they were being imported from abroad. Millions of dollars were spent paying men to slaughter millions of pigs, while we increased our imports of lard. Corn production was cut down as we imported 30 million bushels of corn.

The top one percent of the farmers received 21% of the benefits, while farm foreclosure rates hit a high of 38%. Only the war finally rescued the farmers from the New Deal disasters. Yet most Americans believed that FDR's New Deal programs were targeted to help America's poorest! But that was not so. The South, with its high percentage of poor black voters, got relatively little New Deal money, because FDR knew he already had the solidly Democratic Southern vote in his pocket— especially since few poor blacks ever went to the polls.

Powell reveals that in 1969, Utah historian Leonard Arrington ranked all 50 states according to how much New Deal spending they received. The top 14 states were all in the West. In effect, FDR used New Deal money to court the smaller states' electoral votes. Economic historian Gavin Wright has estimated that 80% of the state-by-state variation in per-capita spending could be explained by political factors. In *The Political Economy of The New Deal*, published in 1998, economists Jim Couch and William Shughart analyze New Deal spending patterns.

They believe the evidence suggests that the most important motive underlying FDR's New Deal spending was political self-interest.

Powell points out how the TVA, Social Security, and other FDR programs all contributed to stalling any possible recovery during the Great Depression. He goes on to show how earlier financial disasters were handled in a year or two by allowing the free market to progress normally.

FDR assumed powers unprecedented in American history. And even though Democrats controlled Congress, he issued a total of 3728 Executive Orders, some which contradicted other existing Orders, creating more bureaucratic waste and confusion. These Executive Orders totaled more than all of his successors' combined, through President Clinton.

Under the guise of a national emergency, FDR prolonged the Great Depression because he lacked an understanding of basic economics. He offered nothing more than his own egotistical ideas of class warfare and government control. He trampled on the idea of states' rights and sacrificed individual interests for the good of the collective, believing that he and his small group of "progressives" were best suited to dictate America's future. Individuals and businesses gave up fundamental liberties while the powers of the government were monumentally expanded. Yet it appears that the New Dealers never considered the possibility that more power in the hands of the government could magnify the harm done by corruption or human error.

I believe FDR lacked the human capacity to care for anyone other than himself, and he treated the American people as guinea pigs in order to pursue his own misguided socialistic theories. His inability to see his wife as anything more than an object to further his own political aspirations was the same fault that led him to disregard the American people as they struggled with hunger and poverty.

In 1936, George Orwell made the statement that the era of history had ended and the era of propaganda had begun. I think he may have had FDR in mind. Looking back at it from today's perspective, I am struck by the irony that after issuing 3728 Executive Orders, many of which contradicted previous Orders, FDR never once admitted to having made any mistakes.

FDR was a Harvard man, and it was well known that most of his close associates and advisers were also from the Ivy League Universities so well known for their "progressive" ideas. Like Wilson, FDR also had a very mysterious aid that he trusted implicitly. Harry Hopkins had been one of FDR's point men on the New Deal, and was the only person that FDR trusted to communicate his most secret assurances to Churchill that he was determined to get into the War. Churchill referred to him as "Lord Root of the Matter." It was also Hopkins who carried secret messages to Stalin, and supervised the lend-lease program that allowed FDR to lend massive amounts of money and war materials to Europe and Russia prior to the U.S. entrance into the war.

In his 1990 book *KGB: The Inside Story*, Oleg Gordievsky, a high level KGB defector describes Hopkins as the most important of all Soviet wartime agents in the U.S. It was over strong opposition that Hopkins was able to persuade an ailing FDR to go to Yalta. It was at Yalta where FDR signed the fate of Poland and much of Eastern Europe, giving them to Stalin and his Communist rule.

The powerful J.P. Morgan stayed in the background as he financed the formation of the Council of Foreign Relations (CFR) in 1921. This private organization was well connected to the privately funded Endowments that supported a one-world government, and had been able to easily infiltrate the U.S. State Department. The CFR began a series of State Department study groups in the early forties that focused on postwar planning for peace and the long-term problems of war. The results of these studies were not made public, but went directly to the State Department and FDR. In his book, *The New World Government*

Exposed, David Montgomery explains that the actions of the CFR briefly raised the concerns of the FBI, which investigated them for connections to Nazi and Communist groups during World War II. However, the investigation was dropped after powerful interests in the U.S, government applied pressure on the FBI.

Alger Hiss was also an undercover Soviet agent and advisor to FDR. He was head of the State Department's Post-War Foreign Policy Planning Division. He also became the President of the Carnegie Endowment Fund, which strongly supported the United Nations, and was the very first Secretary General of the U.N. It would be in 1954 that Rowan Gaither, President of the Ford Foundation, would reveal to Norman Dodd that many tax-exempt organizations were using grant money to study ways to affect policies intended to alter life in the U.S. Dodd was the chief investigator for the Congressional Committee to investigate tax-exempt foundations. Gaither admitted that their goal was to merge the two great superpowers into one, under the umbrella of the United Nations.

There are strong connections between the Order of Skull and Bones, a secret society established at Yale University in 1833, the CFR, and several other groups that we will examine in later chapters.

8

THE FIRST CASUALTY OF WAR IS TRUTH

In his book *Death By Government*, R. J. Rummel cites statistics of the people murdered by governments prior to World War II. By 1939, the USSR, under Stalin, had conquered 16% of the earth's surface and murdered 42.6 million innocent civilians. China, under Chiang Kai-Chek, had murdered 10.2 million people. By 1939 the French Empire was well established, and the British had conquered 22% of the earth's land surface. Both the French and the British had killed untold millions in the prior century as they expanded their empires. These were our allies.

Germany, under Hitler, murdered almost 21 million people, of which six million were Jews. Japan murdered almost six million people. These were our enemies. It is easy to say Hitler was a brutal menace, but was he really any worse than Stalin, whom we supported? Based on the writings of Karl Marx, it was the Soviet Socialists who were intent on conquering the world. Richard Maybury, in his book *World War II: The Rest of the Story*, points out that the war was primarily one between Germany and Russia, between fascists and socialists.

In August, 1939, Germany and Russia signed a nonaggression pact. Hitler invaded Poland on September 1, 1939, which started the war against Germany. But almost no mention is ever made of the fact that on September 17, Stalin too invaded Poland, from the other side! Then, on November 30th, he attacked Finland, and on June 17, 1940, he conquered Latvia, Lithuania, and Estonia. And prior to 1940 he had conquered Kazakhstan, a state far larger than anything Hitler ever managed to steal. Now France and Germany got into the war because they had signed alliance pacts with Poland. In the center of it all, the Swiss stayed neutral.

The Battle of Britain was fought in the summer and fall of 1940, with the English fighter planes emerging victorious. The Germans would occasionally bomb England after this, but only in halfhearted attempts, since an invasion was no longer feasible. Why? England is an island, and Germany needed to capture a port to unload their supplies. Possessing none of the Higgins boats we would later use to land on the beaches of Normandy, the Germans could not land an invasion party. All the same, both Britain and France felt vulnerable because their fleets were already busy protecting their colonial holdings.

On June 22, 1941, Hitler made a mistake that even his generals knew would be fatal: he decided to attack Russia. Genghis Khan had been the only person able to invade Russia during the winter months. He had done this in 1236, and it had taken him four years. On September 12, 1941, just three months after Hitler's attack on Russia, the first snow began to fall, spelling the end of Hitler's invasion. For the next four years, any German soldier sent to the Eastern Front knew it was a death sentence.

When Franklin Roosevelt ran for President in 1940, he campaigned with the promise that he would not send American boys into any foreign wars. On June 24th, 1941, he announced that he was siding with Stalin. Four months before Pearl Harbor, the polls showed that 80% of the Americans wanted no part in the fighting that had been going on in Europe. The memory of World War I was still fresh.

Roosevelt had anticipated this when he hired Frank Capra, a favorite Hollywood film director, to make propaganda war movies favoring American intervention in the war. Two film series were produced, *Why We Fight* and *Victory At Sea*. They painted a rousing picture of the good guys fighting the bad guys to victory, and were considered quite successful.

On August 9, 1941, off the coast of Newfoundland, Winston Churchill and President Roosevelt met in what was called the Atlantic Charter Conference. In his book *And I Was There*, Edwin T. Layton states that FDR and Churchill reached a de facto agreement that would bring the United States into the war if Britain were attacked. This violated not only our Constitution, but also the Neutrality Act, which Congress had passed and Roosevelt had signed.

In early 1940, Lieutenant Commander Arthur H. McCollum was placed in charge of all intelligence about Japan that was sent to Roosevelt. He believed the Americans should join the war against Germany by goading the Japanese into attacking U.S. Navy ships. He drew up and circulated an eight-point plan that is outlined in *Day of Deceit* by Robert B. Stinnett. This plan included sending the U.S. fleet to Hawaii from San Diego, cutting off all British, Dutch, and American oil supplies to Japan, and aiding China, Japan's enemy. It was known that Secretary of War Henry Stimson favored the plan.

Maybury details how Roosevelt put this plan into action in 1940 and 1941. Admiral Richardson, who strongly objected to these tactics, was fired by Roosevelt in February, 1941, and replaced by Admiral Kimmel. Behind the scenes, FDR was funding Britain and Russia and forming the Flying Tigers in China. The U.S. government intercepted a message on October 9 showing that Pearl Harbor was to be hit. But no one told Admiral Kimmel.

On November 23, Kimmel knew something was up and went out looking for the Japanese, but was ordered back to Hawaii by FDR. He was then ordered to send all of his modern warships away from Hawaii. On December 1, 1941, Hong Kong and Britain declared a state of emergency in preparation for an expected Japanese attack. A Congressional investigation revealed in 1946 that Navy headquarters had ordered 21 of the most modern ships in the 7th Fleet to leave Pearl Harbor and deploy at Wake and Midway Islands, just days before the December 7th attack. When the Japanese arrived at Pearl Harbor, all they found were the old relics from World War I. Admiral Kimmel and Lieutenant Commander Short had been set up to take the blame for Pearl Harbor.

On March 9, 1945, an American bomber squadron of 279 B-29s attacked Tokyo. These bombings killed 185,000, more than the total at Hiroshima and Nagasaki combined. This took six hours. By August of that year we had Japan completely blockaded. Navy Under Secretary Ralph Bard was convinced we could sit and wait for Japan to collapse.

But the U.S. government wanted to try out its new weapon, so the decision was made to bomb Hiroshima "to save American lives." 75 hours later, another atomic bomb was dropped on Nagasaki, even though U.S. leaders knew the Japanese were in the process of surrendering.

General Leslie R. Groves was the head of the Manhattan Project. In his book *Now It Can Be Told*, he reports that on July 22, 1943, Churchill expressed "vital concern" about the need to intimidate the Russians, our allies at the time. President Truman's journal, discovered in 1979, made it clear that the purpose of dropping the atomic bombs was to send a message of power to Russia.

In 1992, James Sanders, Mark Sauter, and R. Cort Kirkwood revealed another of FDR's dark secrets in their well-documented book, *Soldiers of Misfortune: Washington's Secret Betrayal of American POWs in the Soviet Union.* It tells of the agreement made by Stalin, Churchill, and FDR to return soldiers that had been captured by the Germans. But by the time the war ended, the U.S. government had already begun to mistrust and demonize the Russians. Hardly the trusting type himself, Stalin held back thousands of U.S. and British prisoners. He then carted them off—20,000 American and over 30,000 British soldiers—to the Russian *gulag*, where they spent the rest of their lives.

Many Americans still have difficulty believing that a man considered one of our great Presidents could have done anything so horrible as to sacrifice American soldiers to get into the war. But it was well known that FDR had an intense hatred for the Japanese. He considered them barbarians. It is only thanks to the Freedom of Information Act that scholars such as Stinnett, who spent more than 50 years researching his book, have been able to dig up this previously secret information.

In an article entitled "Covering the Map of the World" published in *The Failure of America's Foreign Wars*, Richard Ebeling gives many insightful descriptions of FDR's behavior and his attitude toward Stalin. Either FDR was so intoxicated with images of his own power and infallibility that he thought he could outwit the devil (Stalin), or he just admired him and wanted to be like him as much as possible. As he once told an assistant, "What helps a lot is that Stalin is the only man I have to convince. Joe doesn't worry about a Congress or a Parliament. He's the whole works."

Thus the U.S. government ended up defeating Hitler only to create a much larger monster in the Soviet Union. Stalin killed more than 42 million civilians before the war, and maybe as many more after. The U.S. government spent billions of dollars dueling with the Soviets during the Cold War because of FDR's egomaniacal folly. I believe that FDR, who had failed to end the Great Depression, was desperate for political power and recognition. He knew that winning a war and saving Europe would give him what he wanted.

Had FDR stayed out of World War II, the entire world would have been better off. We would not have lost thousands at Pearl Harbor, nor would we have sacrificed Hiroshima and Nagasaki to impress the Soviets with our military might. And 20,000 Americans would not have been lost to the Russian *gulag*.

In October of 2000, the United States Congress absolved both Admiral Kimmel and Commander Short of all responsibility for what happened at Pearl Harbor.

The American people did not start out hating the Filipinos or the Germans, any more than they did the Koreans or the Vietnamese. But our politicians have become masters of manipulation, and they use the media to play on our fears and insecurities. Once in office, the majority of them become addicted to their political power. And wars are the ultimate expression of that power. I think it is safe to say that the large majority of Americans want nothing more than to enjoy their lives and families without having to worry about whether their sons and daughters are going to be sacrificed in a foreign land before they reach 25 years of age. When it comes to foreign policy, I believe we would do well to honor Maybury's second precept: Do no encroach on other persons or their property. This, coupled with a desire to stay neutral in world politics, could go a long way toward avoiding self-destruction.

In war there are seldom any true winners, for the victor has almost certainly gained more enemies than he had when he started. We, the United States of America, have been blessed with a country rich in natural resources. We have not come anywhere near reaching our potential, but unless we can come together and take back our government, the American Dream will cease to exist.

It is my personal belief that FDR was a *malignant narcissist*, and I will discuss this in chapter 21. But there are additional facts that may shed even more light on Roosevelt's character and the nature of his mission. Again, they point to something sinister and foreboding.

9

A NEW VISION FOR AMERICA

I have come to believe that the greatest ability of mankind is our ability to utilize our creative imagination. My friend Ed, who lives in New England and has researched this subject quite extensively, says that genius is really just highly developed imagination, and that the more often we exercise it, the more creative and productive we become.

The traditional view of genius is correlated to IQ. But Ed's nontraditional view is based on a results-oriented philosophy that states that since our ability to imagine is boundless, so is our ability to solve our problems. And whether you believe this ability to be a function of Higher Self or a gift from God doesn't matter, for it works the same in either case. All the most successful people have achieved this status because they were able to view their problems from a different perspective than their peers. They are more creative problem solvers.

Our Founding Fathers were critical thinkers, able to analyze a problem logically and thoughtfully. How else could they have founded a nation that has prospered this long? So if we can combine our ability for critical thinking with our creative imagination, we should be able to solve any problem that confronts us.

Among the major religions, only Judaism teaches critical thinking skills to their children. As they study the Torah, their holy book, from an early age, Jewish children are taught to develop their critical thinking skills as they encounter life's difficulties. They are given thought-provoking challenges in which they are required to choose between a variety of viewpoints to determine right from wrong. This may be one reason Jews have prospered in America. There is no doubt that critical thinking skills are vital to the success of any nation.

As we go through life we are constantly changing in one way or another. We change from a child into an adolescent, and then into an adult. We become a reflection of all our thoughts and dreams, our hopes and expectations. Any emotion, positive or negative, held for a long period of time, will sink into our cells and our being. It will be reflected in our face, in our smile, in our eyes.

This is one reason why many people believe we should always let go of negative feelings and emotions as soon as possible. If the negativity lingers too long in our consciousness, it will become a part of us, and then it will begin to cloud the way we experience life. And like water seeking its own level, whatever we hold in our heart determines the type of people we will attract into our lives.

On a national scale, I believe the same holds true. The longer we sit and allow our politicians to take advantage of the system, the more oppressive the weight becomes. We may not notice it ourselves, but each successive generation will feel more burdened by feelings of helplessness and despair. The longer we tolerate the corruption of our politicians, the more hopeless we feel and the harder it becomes to effect change.

There is no doubt in my mind that our two political parties do everything in their power to keep third parties out of the race, unless of course the third party will hurt their opponent. But the fact is that the two parties are both corrupt. What we really have is two groups of power junkies dedicated to one thing—getting reelected—and they have thrown out all thought for the American people. Their platforms are only used to make their sales pitch, and this is adjusted by their spin-doctors, who always have one eye on the tracking polls.

In the 2004 election, the candidates ignored most states as they fought for about eight percent of the registered voters. They ignored the critical issues, such as the deficit and border security, our first line of defense against terrorism. The final election tab was $4.1 billion. Yet, as John Fund points out in his book, *Stealing Elections*, the debates were rigged to serve the two candidates, with no regard to informing the public. We can and should do much better. After all, an open and honest election system is at the very heart of the American Dream. It is what this country was founded on—equal and honest representation. But the power junkies no longer care!

With this in mind, I am going to suggest a very simple solution to the problem of our leaders being too addicted to their power to function as effective legislators. Since they spend so much time raising money to be reelected, it seems only natural that we should try and take the money out of the equation. The easiest way to do this would be to change the way we elect our President.

The largest single expenditure in the race for President is the cost of TV advertising. I propose we eliminate the primary system and allow all candidates who can get a million signatures endorsing their candidacy to run for President. Then we can have a series of debates around the country, nationally televised on the Discovery Channel or the Education Channel, with the government paying the bill. After several debates we can have a national election, which will be held on the weekend, and narrow the field to the seven candidates who get the most electoral votes. Then each of them can choose a running mate and receive minimal government funding for a small staff.

We can then repeat the process with another series of debates and have another Saturday and Sunday election, narrowing the field to the three candidates with the highest Electoral College vote totals. We can repeat the process a third time, and if no one gets the necessary Electoral College majority, we can eliminate the candidate with the lowest total and hold a final election.

This system would also work for members of Congress. It will take a little more time than our current system, but it will be well worth it. Each state could require a candidate for the Senate to get 250,000 signatures to be on the ballot, or 100,000 to be on the ballot for the House of Representatives. There would be a series of debates and several Saturday and Sunday elections to narrow the field and select the eventual winner.

Reinstating term limits would also be a good idea, for it would further discourage career politicians, who tend to think of themselves as American royalty. Our forefathers did not want to create anything close to a royal family. When George Washington was offered such a position shortly after his victory over the British, he declined. Our Founding Fathers believed that serving your government was a noble thing, but they did not believe it should become a career.

I know most people will laugh at such an idea, so I don't expect much to come of it. The most vociferous opponents will be the two parties, for this system would eliminate all or most of the sound bites, lies, and distortion from the campaigns. The privately funded 527s that produced so much propaganda in 2004 would be outlawed. This system would force the candidates to talk openly and honestly about their ideas and goals. And it would be possible because the networks, wanting to contribute to a fair system (ha ha), would accept the advertising rate designated by a national election committee.

We now have the technology to allow electronic voting from our home computers on a standardized system throughout the United States. We can use our ATM cards in every state and many foreign countries, so why can't we make voting just as simple? The problem here is that it would be much easier to rig an electronic election.

The sad truth is that we all know the politicians will fight tooth and nail to maintain their grip on power. Yet if adopted, my system would offer the American people a much better opportunity to hear and understand what the candidates really stand for. True, it would also require more participation for each individual citizen. But the end result would be worth it, for without party cronyism our politicians would have to focus on the issues and would be more likely to follow through with their promises. If we do not change the way we elect our politicians, we will never be able to take back our government. And then we can kiss the American Dream good bye once and for all.

I am floating this idea to demonstrate that by using our creative imagination, along with a little determination and some common sense, we can solve our problems and reach our potential. We the people, the voters, have to find a way to save the American Dream. The answer can only be found by working together, by focusing on a common goal.

We are the most productive democracy the world has ever known, but we are on the verge of collapse. Our house is in chaos, our debt grows larger every day, and our leaders are in denial. Our Department of Defense is spending billions of dollars trying to build a democracy in Iraq, focusing its crosshairs on Syria and Iran, while our borders remain unsecured and vulnerable.

The difference between a visionary and a dreamer is that the visionary has the energy and drive to make the dream come true. We need to fully utilize our powers of creative imagination to make our visions of the future become a reality.

Election reform is one of the critical issues I will focus attention on at my web site. I invite you to join me as an American Eagle Member at www.uniteamericanow.com.

PART II

Whoever controls the volume of money in our country is absolute master of all industry and commerce... and when you realize that the entire system is very easily controlled, one way or another, by a few powerful men at the top, you will not have to be told how periods of inflation and depression originate.

—President James Garfield
several weeks before he was assassinated on July 2, 1881

10

ISLAND JEKYLL AND MR. HYDE

As a nation we are much concerned about the strength of our economy. We were able to become the financial superpower of the world because our free enterprise system was based on Common Law. Each person was aware of the rules and could depend upon the stability of our laws and regulations to plan ahead, to invest in the future, and to build for our families. To this end it is in our best interest to have a stable money supply.

Yet we are fast approaching a financial crisis. Our infrastructure is decayed, our politicians are corrupt, and the welfare system has us on the edge of disaster, headed the way of Rome. If we the people don't stand up and demand a change it may soon be too late. We may not have much time to reverse the situation.

Our population is aging rapidly, with the baby boomer generation fast approaching retirement age, while the fertility rates in this country have been decreasing for many years. Several factors have contributed to this trend, including the birth control pill and our more affluent life style. The current birth rate is at 2.2 children per woman, which is about the rate required to sustain a population.

Based on the latest census, predictions are that between 2000 and 2040, the number of people aged 65 to 74 will increase by about 85%, but the population over 85 will increase by about 225%. Peter G.

Peterson, in his book *Running On Empty,* points out that as recently as the 1960s there were 5.1 working taxpayers for every person receiving Social Security. Currently the figure is down to 3.3, and by 2030 it is projected to be down to 2.2.

By the year 2040, Social Security outlays as a percentage of worker payroll will rise from 11.1 to 17.8, while Medicare will rise from 5.6% to 18.2%. And the total bill for federally funded entitlements, which now amounts to 12.5% of our Gross Domestic Product (GDP), will increase to 21.7% of GDP. If the birth rate continues to fall, the costs to pay for Social Security and Medicare would naturally be higher for each working person. If the birth rate were to fall to 1.7 children per woman, we would have to tax away 56.7% of our workers' payroll to fund these liabilities.

Technology has proven to be a blessing, but also a potential curse. The MRI, open-heart transplants, and other innovations have added to the number of years we live. Unfortunately, this has resulted in rapidly increasing medical costs. On average, older Americans consume nearly four times the medical services used by a younger adult, and about seven times as much as a child. Medical expenditures over the average lifetime are heavily weighted toward the end of life. Approximately 90% of an individual's lifetime healthcare costs will occur in the last year, often with little or no increase in the quality of life. In fact, the last year is often marked by increased pain, discomfort, and suffering.

One of the largest problems is our unfunded liability: the future guarantees for Social Security, Medicare, and Medicaid. These benefits, which millions of Americans are expecting to receive, are projected to amount to as much as $70 trillion by the middle of the century. Social Security benefits are likely to be reduced, and the age at which one can begin to receive benefits is likely to be extended. The Social Security trust fund does not actually have any money in it, but rather is filled with IOUs. As soon as funds come in, they are used to meet other obligations and then replaced with another IOU.

President Bush's attempt to privatize a part of the Social Security system is being criticized by the Democrats, who feel that privatizing the system is too costly and offers very little benefit. Peterson points out that the Social Security system is basically a government-run Ponzi scheme that benefits older workers at the expense of younger workers.

Here again we find that the reforms instituted by FDR as he socialized the American economic landscape have returned to haunt us. This program did absolutely nothing to diminish the Great Depression and is today a bureaucratic mess. Any solution put forward by either party will fall far short of solving the real problem, but then that has never stopped our politicians.

Some might suggest that we simply need to grow the economy. Peterson points out that overly optimistic projections for growth usually fall short of expectations. Also, Social Security benefits are indexed to wages, so when productivity goes up, revenues go up—but average benefits (and the taxes that support them) also go up.

Balancing our budget will mean taking on the national entitlement programs, which account for two-thirds of our federal budget. When George Bush took office, he commissioned a study on Social Security. But the results were so daunting that he chose to ignore the findings of his own commission. President Clinton did the exact same thing.

Peterson discounts two possible solutions, immigration and inflation (we will look at the issue of immigration in chapter 12). He does not want to accept inflation as the solution to the problem because this cure is usually worse than the problem. I agree that inflating our way out of the problem would be a mistake. However, since it takes little or no courage to inflate our way out of the debt, that is probably what our politicians will do. The financial markets have already recognized that this has been happening for some time now, as the dollar has lost a third of its value against the euro in the last couple of years. We are probably going to suffer a hard and rather unpleasant landing.

One thing that is very little understood is the role of the Federal Reserve Bank, which is supposed to monitor inflation. The Fed is not actually a part of the federal government and has very little incentive to keep a lid on inflation. The Federal Reserve System is accountable to no one. It has no budget, it is subject to no audit, and no Congressional committee knows of or can truly supervise its operations.

It is sadly ironic that we micro-manage the labels on all of our food products, yet the Federal Reserve, which influences every aspect of our economy, has complete and total freedom to do as it pleases. The Federal Reserve Bank of New York is a private institution owned by its shareholders, a conglomeration of banks. According to the Board of Governors, two banks now own over 60% of this organization: J.P. Morgan Chase owns a little over 40% of the shares and Citibank owns around 20.5%.

Murray N. Rothbard explains the history of the Fed in his book, *The Case Against the Fed*. At its inception, the United States of America established a Central Bank, but that bank was dissolved after 20 years. America was more in favor of free markets and a gold-backed system of banking, which was not as favorable to the Rothschilds. The Rothschilds then agreed to finance the War of 1812 in hopes that England could win back the colonies. This would greatly increase their opportunities for profit.

Because this war failed to bring the United States back under British control, the Rothschilds created a secret society called the Knights of the Golden Circle (KGC), which would eventually mutate into the Ku Klux Klan. A second Central Bank was formed in 1816. However, in the 1830s Andrew Jackson disbanded it once again, calling the bankers a den of thieves and vipers. This appears to have been aimed at the House of Rothschild.

During the Civil War the Rothschilds attempted to forge a divide between the North and the South as the KGC infiltrated Lincoln's Cabinet. The French, British, and Spanish sent troops to Mexico to launch an assault from the south, while the British also had a force prepared to enter from Canada. However, Lincoln prevailed upon the Russian Czar, Alexander II, to position part of his fleet off of New York and the rest of his fleet off the coast of California. Alexander made it very clear that he would join the North if the French, British, or the Spanish attacked from either side. This came back to haunt Russia, for the House of Rothschild remembered this deed and later helped to overthrow the Czar by fomenting the Russian Revolution in 1917.

The bank reform movement began again in 1896 with the support of two powerful competitors, the Rockefellers and J.P. Morgan. Normally fierce rivals, these two groups conspired to reestablish the Central Banking System because it offered more *elasticity*, which was their word for inflation. They put together a pseudo-grass-roots organization that promised to protect the public from the manipulations of the big bankers, and then waged a sophisticated propaganda campaign as "enlightened and progressive protectors" of the public interest. They established commissions staffed by the media and other "impartial experts" to insure that the public was getting a fair shake.

The major thrust of the central bank movement began in 1910 on Jekyll Island, which was a private club in the Atlantic Ocean off Glynn County, Georgia. It was used by an elite group of Wall Street financiers for their private deal making. Five influential bankers that had been hand picked by J.P. Morgan to write the language for a bill to create a new Central Bank joined Senator Nelson Aldrich. The bankers were very wealthy and Senator Aldrich was the father-in-law of John D. Rockefeller, Jr. It was absolutely essential that Congress and the public remain in the dark about this meeting, or the measure would face severe opposition.

In fact, the bill was defeated in 1910, but the bankers had not played their last card. Cleveland Dodge, a banking powerhouse of the times, sponsored Woodrow Wilson for the Presidency of Princeton University in the early 1900's. Wilson demonstrated his support for the elite bankers and was again sponsored by them to be Governor of New Jersey in 1910. In the background all along, Colonel House tapped Wilson for the upcoming presidential election of 1912. Wilson campaigned as a candidate who opposed the trusts and monopolies and favored the Sherman Anti-Trust Act. Shortly after his victory and inauguration, the banking elite reintroduced the legislation that had originated on Jekyll Island. Wilson sponsored this bill through Congress as a currency reform bill.

The Republican minority was not allowed to examine the final conference report, and there was extensive lobbying that the bill not be amended or tampered with at all. Wilson signed the bill into law and thus was transferred the control of the American money supply from Congress to the Global Elite. They now had full control to manipulate the United States money supply without government intervention or criticism. To this day criticism of the Federal Reserve System is squashed to a minimum, and dissenters are labeled as heretics. This transfer of power is one of the more disgraceful and unconstitutional perversions of American government in our history.

The first act of the Federal Reserve was to double the money supply by lowering the reserve requirements. World War I started shortly thereafter. It is generally agreed that it was this new central banking system that allowed the U.S. to pay for its own war effort and to also finance the massive loans to our allies. Shortly after the war started, the House of Morgan became the sole materials purchasing agent for the U.S., France, and Britain. It also became sole underwriter for the bonds the British and the French floated in the United States. I am of the opinion that the assassination that started World War I was part of a plan by the international banking elite to increase their wealth and spread their influence even farther.

The Rockefellers had long been allies of the House of Rothschild, which once again was making substantial profits from war in Europe. Another group that will always benefit from warfare are the munitions makers, and the Rockefellers were well on their way to becoming one of the world's dominant munitions makers. The wartime measures allowed the Fed to permanently centralize the American gold supplies in their own hands. At the same time, they were able to nationally coordinate their inflation policies while they weaned Americans from the daily use of gold in their lives.

The early years of the Federal Reserve System (the name was chosen to imply that it was part of the government) were dominated by the House of Morgan, though Rockefeller finally took control, possibly because of his long time alliance with the House of Rothschild. The Rockefellers used their coalition and the New Deal Banking Acts to shift the crucial balance of power from Wall Street, Morgan, and the New York Fed to the politicos in Washington D.C.

Alan Greenspan was affiliated with the Morgan Guaranty Trust Company before he became Chairman of the Fed. His predecessor, Paul Volker, received his undergraduate degree from Princeton, his M.A. from Harvard, and did post graduate work at the London School of Economics. Volker's first job was with the Federal Reserve and over the next 30 years he divided his time between the Fed and the major banking institutions on the U.S. This "revolving door" policy has helped to blur the distinctions between his public and private service, which is to the benefit of the semi-secret organizations to which he belongs.

Our Constitution designated that the U.S. Treasury be responsible for issuing our money, but it is the Federal Reserve that now controls monetary policy and the pace of inflation. The Federal Reserve Bank has long maintained that it is by virtue of its independence from the government and the accompanying political affiliations that it is able to be effective in setting monetary policy. Whether or not this is true, it does not come anywhere close to telling the real story.

It is time for all Americans to speak up and be heard and demand that our politicians act with the same sense of fiscal responsibility they expect of us. The bottom line is that we have to take action now or risk very serious consequences in the near future. Quite literally, if we remain silent much longer we will be flushing our children's American Dream right down the toilet.

11

INFLATION: BANKRUPTING AMERICA

Many Americans have a limited understanding of inflation, and have never seen the damage it can do, though we may get that opportunity in the near future. As much as I like the idea of cutting taxes, it is hard to understand how Bush is going to pay for the war in Iraq without making the necessary budget cuts. However, there is one group who does have a money printing monopoly, the Federal Reserve. So it is essential to understand who really controls the Fed and what motivation they have, if any, to control inflation.

As the Roman Empire expanded, it raised taxes regularly to pay for the many expenses of building an empire, including the military campaigns waged in foreign lands. Taxing means taking money by force, and those who don't pay taxes usually face stiff penalties. It got to the point that the taxes were so high that Rome dared not raise them any further. But still they needed money. And that was when they discovered counterfeiting.

The main coin used in Roman times was the *denarius*, which was 940-fine silver, or 94% silver. When the tax collectors returned with the coins they had collected, the Roman government started clipping or shaving the edges off of the coins. These shavings were used to mint new coins that had non-precious metal added in to increase the amount of money they put back into circulation.

By 218 A.D. the denarius was down to 43% silver, according to Richard Maybury in his book *Whatever Happened to Penny Candy?* 50 years later it contained less than one percent silver. In 100 A.D. a bushel of wheat cost three *denarii*, but by 344 A.D. it cost two million. This was because the politicians wouldn't stop debasing their currency by counterfeiting. Most people today believe that inflation means rising prices, when in fact it really means the value of the currency is falling. The cost of bread didn't go up because it became more precious, but because the *denarius* became so worthless.

In 1270 Kublai Khan wanted silver and gold very badly, so he began writing "20 Ounces of Gold" on a piece of paper and signing his name. People were hesitant to accept this paper money until he passed a legal tender law, which said that those who refused to take this money would be punished. Since Kublai Khan could be a bit of a brute, the people decided to accept his legal tender money. The French government did the same thing in the 1790s, printing phony money and instituting a legal tender law. Refuse to accept it for trade or services? Off with your head!

The Treaty of Versailles forced a severe depression onto the German people. The only way Germany could stay alive was to print more money, and still many thousands starved to death. This is what caused the hyperinflation of the 1920s, the reason a pound of butter went from three marks in 1918 to six trillion marks five years later. Most historians agree that this extreme poverty and the resulting anger of the German people was what opened the door of opportunity to Hitler's propaganda.

The end of World War II saw a monumental change in the way the world conducted its financial affairs. In 1944, at Bretton Woods, NH, it was determined that the dollar would be the standard by which all of the other world currencies would be calibrated. The price of the dollar was fixed at $35 per ounce of gold. America agreed that any nation in the world could come to the U.S. with dollars and exchange them for gold, at $35 per ounce. The House of Morgan played a decisive though behind-the-scenes role in the Bretton Woods Agreement, which they presented to the U.S. government at the end of the war, *fait accompli.*

John Maynard Keyes and Harry Dexter White were also involved in the Bretton Woods agreement. White worked for Treasury Secretary Morgenthau. The stated purpose of the agreement was to provide monetary stability and facilitate international trade and the free flow of capital around the world. The International Monetary Fund (IMF) was established to monitor the system and provide bridge loans to nations facing a run on their currencies. The U.S. then transferred 104 million ounces of gold and billions of dollars of cash into the new International Monetary Fund to get it rolling.

The World Bank, a sister institution of the IMF, was also developed at this time to provide loans to countries trying to recover from the war. The U.S. supplanted England as the financial giant of the world and virtually guaranteed the recovery of the enemies we had defeated. The financial strain of this system wasn't really felt until Lyndon Johnson tried to fund the war in Vietnam and the Great Society at the same time. Finally, in August of 1971 Nixon took us off the gold standard, letting the dollar float and allowing all of the world's currencies to seek their own level.

Up until about 1965, the dollar bill bore the phrase *Silver Certificate*, which meant it was redeemable for one dollar in silver. But because the Federal Reserve kept printing so many of them, they no longer had the gold and silver reserves to back them up. That's when the phrase was changed to say "Federal Reserve Note," which simply meant that it was an IOU based on faith and trust in the U.S. Government. Until the 1930s gold coins were allowed to circulate, and until the 1960s silver coins actually had silver in them. Now they are just tokens representing IOUs.

Not so surprisingly, inflation has almost no negative effect on the members of the Federal Reserve System. The assets of the Fed fall into two major categories. The first is the gold, which was confiscated from the public under FDR and later amassed by the Fed. The liabilities of the Fed are no longer redeemable in gold. The Fed safeguards its gold by depositing it with the Treasury and getting *gold certificates* that are guaranteed to be backed one hundred percent by gold. Yet the Fed's creditors must accept the fiat money that has been losing its value over the course of many decades.

The Fed's other major asset is the total of the U.S. government securities it has purchased and amassed over the years. When the Fed wants to increase the money supply by $9 billion (assuming that the reserve requirement is 10%), it writes out a check on itself for one billion dollars, out of thin air, and uses this to purchase securities from a bond dealer, such as Goldman Sachs. Goldman Sachs then deposits the check in its account and is able to lend out $9 billion dollars against the one billion it deposited. This costs the Federal Reserve absolutely nothing.

This is a very simple explanation of how the money supply gets expanded. But the fact is that there is no incentive for the Fed to be inflation hawks. We have put the fox in charge of the hen house. The Fed is the problem. Murray Rothbard contends that since 1914 our periods of inflation have been more intense, and our depressions far deeper, than ever before. He suggests that we use the 260 million ounces of gold the Fed is holding to pay off our liabilities. It is currently valued at $42.22 an ounce, and he recommends that we revalue it at whatever figure it takes to pay off our debt, and then use that figure as the basis for fixing a price for the dollar. This would put us back on the gold standard and a more stable footing.

Further, Rothbard believes we should then eliminate the Fed and cancel the hundreds of billions of dollars of Treasury Notes it holds, relieving the taxpayer of these liabilities and the interest payments.

Rothbard's book was written in 1994, and he died the following year. Although the Federal debt has grown substantially since then, his ideas still have merit today and would go a long way toward eliminating the federal debt.

Along with some other changes in our political system, this would be a good first step is getting America back on the right track. The Founding Fathers were aware of the history of inflation, and so in the Constitution, Article 1, Section 10, it says, "No State shall make any….. Thing but gold and silver Coin a Tender in Payment of Debts." They did this to prevent history from being repeated.

The Roman government had projects much the same as ours: building roads and bridges, welfare, and wars. A welfare program is the means by which money is given to poor people; money given to rich people is called a subsidy. In the last chapter we discussed Social Security, but most economists realize that Medicare is an even bigger problem. These programs are fraught with fraud and waste, yet our politicians continue to spend money like drunken sailors. The longer they delay reform, the bigger the fallout. And it won't be the members of the Federal Reserve who get hurt, but the average person on the street.

When politicians make ever-bigger promises to get reelected, it is a sure sign that the decline has begun and the end is on the horizon. Rome's golden period lasted two hundred years. Our government is about 225 years old, and we may have passed our zenith. Most economists have known for a long time that debasing a nation's currency is a sure road to disaster. However, there is one group that always profits, and that is the Federal Reserve Bank.

In 1953 Eisenhower's Attorney General charged ex-President Truman with having known since 196 that Harry Dexter White (who helped to formulate the Bretton Woods plan) was a spy. And the late Senator Pat Moynihan said there was no doubt that Harry Dexter White was a Soviet spy. One has to wonder… why would the U.S. government take on the enormous burden of becoming banker to the world? Why do we really need the Fed? And why should it continue to receive the monstrous interest payments it has saddled upon the American people?

Did the American people even understand what the politicians were doing? Did they know that Communist spies were deciding American financial policies? Did they know the risks this was exposing them to? I would have to think not. We will take another look at the power structure of the Fed in a later chapter. The shadow of those planning for the destruction of the American Dream looms ever larger.

12

THE INVISIBLE INVADERS

It is no secret that for years our politicians have fostered an open border policy. Illegal aliens are crossing the Mexican border at the rate of approximately three million per year, or 8,000 per day. Current estimates put the total number of illegal aliens currently living in the U.S. at 20 million. Yet nobody seems to be very concerned, except a majority of the American public.

The ACLU claims we have no choice but to allow the influx to continue, while the American taxpayer is expected to shoulder this burden, no matter the cost. Many of our politicians refer to illegal aliens as undocumented immigrants, as if there were no problem at all. And President Bush is preparing to give worker status to all illegal aliens, although no one is stupid enough to expect them to return to Mexico when their permits expire. He claims illegal aliens take jobs that Americans won't do, but he ignores the fact that their presence has undermined American wages. In 2004 CNN estimated that illegal aliens have lowered the American wage by five to seven percent over the last few years

In 1996 Bill Clinton gave legal status to six million illegal aliens, rewarding them for having broken our laws. This one-time opportunity was supposed to solve the problem, but nothing was done to close the border with Mexico, and the flow has only increased. Our politicians used a band-aid solution for a serious problem, and now we are approaching a state of crisis. Yet Bush is not even pretending he will close the border.

According to Californians For Population Stabilization (CAPS), 95% of the outstanding homicide warrants and two-thirds of the felony warrants in L.A. are for illegal aliens. In 2002, we spent $2.2 billion on education due to illegal immigration, and $350 million in medical bills were paid by the state. And that was just in L.A. County.

Official Mexican policy supports the flow of illegal aliens across the border. They have established the Office for Mexicans Abroad to provide survival kits to help Mexicans evade U.S. border guards in the deserts of Arizona and California. The Mexican government has been distributing information to help illegal aliens obtain free social services in California, no questions asked. In December, 2004, the Mexican government began publishing this information in comic book form. Yet Bush remains silent.

The money Mexicans send back home represents the second-largest industry in Mexico. Only the oil industry brings in more money. In January, 2005, Lou Dobbs reported the existence of a huge underground economy, much of it comprised of illegal aliens from Mexico. It has been estimated that, if taxed, the additional revenue from the Mexican underground economy could bring in between 100 and 400 billion dollars.

The irony is that Mexico has more billionaires that the U.S., according to information released on December 17, 2004, by Lou Dobbs on CNN. Mexico is happy to export as much of their population as we will take, to help alleviate the tremendous disparity between their rich and their poor. Rather than fixing their morally corrupt government, Mexico wants the United States to bear the burden.

Already Hispanics are the fastest growing segment in America. We have allowed more illegal aliens to enter from Mexico than we can possibly absorb into our culture. Many of them make no attempt to assimilate, unlike past generations of immigrants, and some even claim to be recolonizing America. Some illegal aliens are even claiming that California will become a Mexican state. Their attitude is one of defiance, and they say that if we don't like it we can leave.

The day after the 2004 elections, President Fox of Mexico charged the state of Arizona with discrimination because it passed Proposition 200, which requires that all people who apply for taxpayer benefits prove that they are American citizens. He believes that anyone who cares to cross the border illegally should be supported and cared for by the American taxpayer.

Mexican drug gangs have started shooting at border patrol agents, killing two of them last year. They are the ones responsible for smuggling tens of thousands of illegal aliens and millions of dollars of drugs across the border. Even worse, these gangs are now smuggling young teenage girls across the border, promising to get them Green Cards. Once across the border, they are gang raped, completely broken down mentally and emotionally, and then sold on the streets as prostitutes all across America.

About two years ago, *60 Minutes* televised a show about gangs from Latin America that were systematically robbing shopping malls throughout the U.S. They are sophisticated, and work in teams. One member will act as a decoy while the others rob the store blind. They seldom get caught. If they do get arrested, they have phone numbers to call. They are bailed out immediately, and then they disappear into another American city to start stealing again. The Federal Prosecutor's Office in San Diego recently declared that it is too overburdened to take on any new cases involving illegal aliens.

This is nothing short of an invasion, and our politicians are guilty of abdicating their responsibility on this issue. There is a 14-mile section of fence along the border that separates San Diego from Tijuana, and four miles of it is so broken down that it is useless. Eight years ago Congress voted to fix the fence, but due to minor environmental vegetation issues the repairs have not been completed. The House voted in 2004 to proceed with a new fence, but the Senate voted it down. So every night hundreds, possibly thousands, of illegal aliens cross through the old broken fence into San Diego. Yet in 2004, the federal and state governments gave $9.5 million dollars to Mexican health clinics to ensure that the illegal aliens would bring less disease when they crossed into America.

In October of 2004, D.A. John Morganelli brought charges against 27 illegal aliens in North Hampton, PA. They all pled guilty to a variety of charges that included credit card fraud, identity theft, and several other offenses. Morganelli expected them to at least get some jail time, maybe six months. But Judge Leonard Zito set them all free. His reasoning was that because the Department of Immigration had no plans to detain them, before or after they had served their sentence, he shouldn't have to do its job. Because our federal government failed to do its job, Judge Zito refused to do his, and he released 27 criminals back into society with no punishment.

What would happen if only four or five terrorists decided to enter shopping malls around the country on December 23, at the height of our holiday shopping season, and set off bombs attached to their bodies? It would be nearly impossible to prevent such an attack, and yet the fear this would create across the country would be enormous. The psychic damage would be almost equal to that of 9/11, even though the death toll would probably be significantly lower.

Surprisingly, illegal immigration is probably the easiest of all of our major problems to solve. The solution is clearly spelled out in the United States Constitution, Article IV, Section 4: "The United States shall guarantee to every state in the Union a Republican form of government and protect each of them against invasion."

When Bill Clinton talked about America becoming a third-world country, he dressed it in the fabric of diversity, and said he wasn't going to worry about it. He took this attitude toward terrorism, and we ended up with September 11. We cannot afford this type of attitude any longer, for the borders are our first line of defense against terrorism. The reduction of crime, drug trafficking, and the slave trade of teenage prostitutes will benefit us as well. *But can we convince our politicians to enforce our own laws?*

The inflow of illegal aliens is becoming such a huge problem that Congress has promised to do something in 2005. The Bush guest worker program is an incredible scam, and Bush is ignoring the fact that most Americans are opposed to this false solution. My fear is that Congress will pass his bill and act like all is right with the world. We have to force them to stand accountable.

The problem is that many of our leaders are no longer beholden to the American people. There is a shadow society that wants to see the identity of America dissolve into a sea of obscurity. The more this secret organization can fracture our identity—the more they can divide us—the easier it is for them to defraud us.

In chapter 10, I mentioned that Peterson ignored the obvious, claiming that we would not allow immigration to soar by five hundred percent. He must have been talking about *legal* immigration, because the *illegal* immigration is way over five hundred percent. And he is ignoring the fact that for more than 10 years now, both the Clinton and Bush administrations have done everything they could to encourage illegal immigration. Bush has gone so far as to say that if he lived in Mexico he too would cross the border illegally to come to America, where the minimum wage is more than 10 times what he could earn in Mexico.

Peterson's book *Running On Empty* is well written and researched, yet he tries to convince us not to worry about immigration or inflation. Peterson is a member of the Council on Foreign Relations and the Trilateral Commission, whose secret agenda is to globalize America into one nation under the U.N. Both Clinton and Bush's father are members of these same two organizations. The power behind these groups is greater than that of the President of the United States, but is cloaked in secrecy, and its powers of persuasion are enormous and sophisticated.

13

PUTTING SOME CLOTHES ON THE EMPEROR

Once again I would like to stretch the limits and make some suggestions that would easily solve our border problems and allow us to document almost every illegal alien in America. Once we accomplish this, we will have the time and resources to focus on rooting out the few remaining illegal aliens who refuse to stand up and be counted.

But every program has to start with stopping all illegal aliens from crossing into the United States from Mexico. If we can't stop the flow from Mexico any measures will be temporary, just like the 1996 Amnesty Agreement.

Once the borders are secure, we can allow all employers to come forward and sponsor any employee for immediate citizenship, so long as they can document a 10-year work history. At the same time, we can announce that we will register all illegal aliens who leave the country voluntarily, and let them back in on a first-out, first-in basis. This means that we register them as they leave, and then we determine our needs. Those who registered earliest can come back soonest. Perhaps the first million will be let back in immediately and given Green Cards and an agreement that they can apply for citizenship in three years. The next two million might be allowed to return with Green Cards and apply for citizenship in five years.

Next, we must begin enforcing the law that penalizes anyone who employs an illegal alien, no exceptions allowed. This will stimulate employers to obey the law. (What a concept!) Then we will be able to determine exactly what our needs are and which countries our immigration quotas will favor.

Immigration has always been a privilege we granted to people from other countries, and it should remain that way. As Ronald Reagan once said, if you cannot control your borders, you are no longer a country. The National Guard is highly qualified to oversee this entire process, and would be better used this way than in Iraq.

I know that some will say this will be a difficult task. I disagree. It will only be difficult if the politicians balk and throw up roadblocks to stop it from interfering with their political agenda, which means their campaign fund-raising. But we have to wean them from their political drugs, because they will never do it unless we force them.

We need to establish an overall ceiling for legal immigration, even for refugees. Then we can determine how many immigrants we want to allow every year, or as conditions warrant. We need to end the chain migration of relatives, which, like a pyramid scheme, swells immigration numbers over time. We need to end the "anchor" provision that allows a woman to sneak across the border and give birth so that her child will be an American citizen. This disincentive alone should help. We need to end the visa lottery, and instead admit people on their merits.

These are measures we have to enact now to prevent America from becoming a third-world country. And we need to make English the legal language. Letting go of our heritage is another way to cloud our memory, to make us forget our American roots. We are the first country founded on an ideal, and our dedication to liberty is to more than the soil beneath our feet. Our politicians have to stop pretending the invaders are here legally.

Currently, hundreds of American cities are struggling to control the problem of illegal aliens. This is costing them millions of dollars in health care bills and destroying their educational systems. Yet both political parties want to ignore the issue because it suits their political agenda. Why won't they put America first? We will look at this in more detail in upcoming chapters.

There is no doubt we are involved in a war, but so far the invaders are not carrying guns—at least we hope not. There have been rumors that al Qaeda is seeking to employ Mexican gangs to help them enter America. We have to win this war, especially because the degradation of our legal system is very alarming. Once the legal protections of our Constitution are eliminated, we will have taken the last step in the decline and fall of the American Dream.

Immigration is another of the critical issues I will focus on at my web site, www.uniteamericanow.com. Please join me as an American Eagle Member and help us spread the word.

14

PAWNING THE AMERICAN DREAM

The Philadelphia convention of 1787 was designed to help the colonies take a critical look at the trade policies of the United States. Thanks to the undeniable influence of George Washington and Benjamin Franklin, a Constitution was born. This new mandate stripped from the states their power to regulate trade, and gave it to Congress. Under President Washington, Congress passed the Tariff Act of 1789, imposing a five percent value-added tax on all goods imported from other countries. This tax was intended to encourage and protect American manufacturers.

In December of 1791, Treasury Secretary Alexander Hamilton clarified that the goal of U.S. trade policy was national self-sufficiency. America would have to stand on its own if it was to maintain its independence. In 1860, Abraham Lincoln owed his election as President largely due to his strong stand in support of tariffs. Between 1865 and 1900, America experienced a golden era of growth and expansion. It wasn't until 1913 that the Sixteenth Amendment became law, and the income tax became a permanent fixture in America. It didn't take long for the income tax to quickly replace tariffs as the primary source of income for the federal government.

After World War II, America threw open her doors to help the countries we had just defeated in the war. This was only meant to be a temporary solution, but Congress never ended the policy and the era of tariffs came to an end. The factories of Germany and Japan were reborn, and their products found their way into our ports. Since then, our dollars have flowed out to them in ever-increasing amounts.

By 1982 the Japanese electronic industry was dominant, and they had been gaining market share in the automobile industry for many years. The Japanese government was strongly supportive, subsidizing many industries with low-interest loans and encouraging them to cooperate in ways forbidden to American industries under our laws. They were caught a number of times engaging in corporate espionage on American corporations, but the penalties were minor. The Japanese government was fighting World War II all over again, only this time it was fighting for economic supremacy.

The Japanese laughed at us as they continued to plunder one industry after another. Most Americans were too busy celebrating their savings to look at what was happening. In 1984 the exchange rate was 350 yen for every dollar. Today the dollar will buy about 103 yen, and the dollar continues to fall. Most Americans don't realize how weak our currency has become. Some have speculated that in 10 years the dollar might only be worth 20% of its current value.

Lou Dobbs, on his TV segment "Exporting America," claims that our manufacturing base has slipped to 11% of the work force and that we are now exporting high-paying service and technology jobs. We are even selling off much of our technology as we export the ability to manufacture many goods essential to our national defense and basic survival.

It is obvious that many members of both parties favor allowing large numbers of illegal aliens to cross the border, hoping it might solve two problems: the issue of the unfunded liabilities from Social Security and Medicare, and the multinationals' need for cheap labor. Our government is trying to hide the truth from the American public.

Multinationals have benefited greatly by having a large pool of low-skilled illegal aliens enter the country, for it allows them to lower their cost of production and makes them more competitive with the foreign corporations in Asia and India. Again, CNN studies show that illegal aliens have lowered the American wage by five to seven percent in the last few years.

In a recent lame duck session, Congress gathered to pass the first Intelligence Reform bill in 40 years. One of the recommendations of the 9/11 Commission was to standardize drivers' licenses and enact a system to document those who are in this country illegally. Given that the 19 terrorists of 9/11 had obtained 63 drivers' licenses, this is a real security issue.

The House favored a provision that would prevent illegal aliens from obtaining drivers' licenses. But the Senate refused to permit inclusion of this provision in the bill. Senator Pat Roberts, a Republican from Kansas, was one of those who fought the hardest to keep this provision out of the Intelligence Reform bill. Why? Agricultural companies depend on low-skilled workers to improve their profits, and research on the Internet showed that according to www.opensecrets.org, Senator Pat Roberts has received approximately $300,000 from agribusiness over the last several years. *Most countries would call such campaign contributions bribes.* The influential Democratic Senator Rockefeller stood firmly with Roberts on this issue.

The argument made by these obstructionists was that it is more important to have safe drivers on our highways than to worry about possible terrorists entering through the open borders. Yet the driver's license has become the de facto means of identifying citizens in our society. The FBI has stated that many of the criminals on our Most Wanted lists are caught when they are stopped for minor traffic violations!

The multinationals have for some time been moving their factories to third-world countries to lower the cost of production and increase their profits. The actual number of jobs exported to foreign countries in the first quarter of 2004 was released in October 2004: approximately 8,200 jobs went to China, 23,000 jobs went to Mexico, and 3,800 jobs went to India. This was the first time these statistics were recorded and available, yet this has been going on for years!

Paul Craig Roberts states in the December 2004 issue of *The American Conservative* that offshore production and job outsourcing benefit the recipient countries and create imports that turn *our* benefits into downward pressure on the dollar as Americans lose income and our trade deficit increases. Our largest trade deficit is with China, whose economy is projected to supplant ours in the near future and become the world's largest. Ironically, the Chinese buy a large portion of the two billion dollars of debt we sell each day to finance our deficit. What would happen if we got into a trade dispute with them and they decided to stop buying our debt?

The rise of our current account deficit over the past three decades is due to our tremendous consumption of foreign goods and our declining national savings rate. As a nation we used to save almost 10% of our earnings. Currently, our savings rate is 0.2%. At this time the Chinese currency is tied to the dollar. As the dollar falls, their exports to us remain constant in value. When the dollar gets too low and they have decimated the competition in certain of our industries, they will allow their currency to rise to its proper level, and the same Chinese imports will cost us double or triple what they do today.

In an article entitled "Losing In A Key Race" for *CBS Market Watch*, December 17, 2004, Marshall Loeb states that in the great global trade competition, the United States is surrendering market share. Foreign producers are catching up with us, and they are not afraid to put restrictions on their own imports, mainly from the U.S. Yet we do nothing to stop the rampant piracy of our entertainment and technology software.

Loeb points to David Wyss, chief economist for Standard and Poor and an expert on this subject. The United States depends largely on taxes on income and production, while the Europeans and many of our competitors depend on sales taxes, notably the value-added tax. But the VAT is not collected on exports. This means that if you produce in the United States and sell in Europe, you are taxed twice! Meanwhile, the European companies joined together to subsidize Airbus, and it has surpassed Boeing as the world leader.

Wyss also discusses education, where he cites dramatic improvement in Japan and Korea. Japan graduates about two engineers for every lawyer we graduate, and in the next generation Asia will graduate more people from college than North America and Europe combined. Recent global studies revealed that the math skills of our 10th-graders rank 24th out of 29 countries around the world, behind Latvia. Sixth from the bottom of the list! Part of the reason for this is that our teachers are overburdened trying to teach students just to read English.

And while we are turning out tens of thousands of engineers each year, the Chinese are turning out millions. And the Chinese have already stated their intention to become the leader in medical research technology. We are about to lose our already decimated textile industry, where a worker makes in a day what the Chinese textile worker makes in a month.

Our trade deficit for November, 2004, was over $60 billion, which means that we bought $60 billion more of other countries' products than they bought from us. We run a trade deficit with almost every country on the planet. It used to be the other way around. But Roberts points out an even more staggering problem. In the eighties our trade deficit was due to oil imports. Today, the trade deficit is in manufactured goods as well as technology, and it is three-and-a-half times the oil import bill.

Currently the dollar continues to act as the reserve currency of the world, primarily because of the size of the U.S. economy and the lack of an alternative. But the European Union's euro has strongly appreciated against the dollar. Also, the depreciation of the dollar negates much of the interest earned by many Asians, and if this trend continues they may stop buying our debt, which will increase the rate of interest we have to pay on our trillions of dollars of debt each year.

The cost of oil has long been tied to the dollar, but this could change, especially if some radical Muslim groups were to gain control of the Middle East oil fields. This could send the value of the dollar plummeting, especially against the cost of a barrel of oil. Were we not burdened by such enormous debts it wouldn't be nearly so painful, though, for we wouldn't be forced to borrow from other governments.

With fewer and fewer alternatives, the more likely choice becomes inflation. During the 1990s our money supply was increased by $2.4 trillion. If the government wants the Fed to inflate our way out of this problem, it could have serious consequences. The politicians will probably be voted out of office when the American people realize how irresponsible they have been, but it will be too late. And the Fed will get richer!

In the year 2000 we raised our debt ceiling to $5.9 trillion. A year or so later the debt ceiling was raised to $6.7 trillion, and in 2004 the debt ceiling was again raised, this time to $7.4 trillion. President Bush recently raised it to $8.2 trillion. And as you know, this does not include the unfunded liabilities. This is truly criminal. But the shadow government is quite happy with this development, for it continually weakens our ability to determine our own future.

What if one day this secret shadow government demanded that we sacrifice some of our Constitutional liberties and become part of a one-world government, with the United States first among equals? In exchange for this they would forgive us all of our debt. I have no doubt that our politicians would sell us out and make the deal in a New York minute. But where would we be a few years later, when *they* wanted to make a favorite son deal with someone else? As the totalitarian force behind a new world government, the Global Elite could do anything they wanted and we would be powerless to stop them!

Because both parties are in denial about their addiction to power, they are willing to say and do almost anything to get reelected. This behavior is similar to that of heroin addicts on the streets of New York, filled with denial and rationalization. Only the fact that the politicians are educated and articulate, with lots of money in the bank, helps them continue their masquerade.

The problem is that they are playing musical chairs with our future. But that doesn't keep them from practicing band-aid politics, hoping that when the storm hits they will not get wet. By then we will have sold off America's assets at fire-sale prices. We will have pawned our children's future and their opportunity to experience the American Dream.

15

POLITICIANS IN WONDERLAND

Early on in the 2004 election, it became apparent that the majority of the population was evenly divided between the Republicans and the Democrats, and it was widely acknowledged that the two political parties were fighting over eight to 10 percent of the voting public. It was also known that in most elections only about half the registered voters turn out to vote. So a great deal of money was spent getting out new voters, as well as trying to solidify the bases of both parties.

In the last three elections almost 98% of the incumbents have kept their seats, because campaigning while already in office is a tremendous advantage. Once elected, their first order of business is to begin working to get reelected. New members are taught how to raise funds for reelection before they have cast a single vote in Congress.

Our Founding Fathers intended Congress to be the first branch of our government. It was the Continental Congress that declared our independence, named George Washington as Commander-in-Chief, engineered the Revolution, sent envoys abroad to negotiate an alliance with France, and then concluded a peace treaty with Britain. The Constitution specifies this hierarchy among the three branches of our government, charging that it is the duty of Congress to authorize spending, regulate foreign trade, and declare war. The Constitution declares all officers of the Executive branch subject to Congressional impeachment, but the members of Congress are answerable only to themselves. The Judiciary was meant to be the smallest branch of government.

But Harry Truman took us to war with Korea calling it a conflict, and 54,000 Americans died there. In Vietnam, without a Declaration of War by Congress, we lost 58,318 soldiers. In the 1990s, Serbia was a European conflict and did not threaten America. The Serbs had already agreed to permit 1,200 U.N. inspectors into Kosovo when President Clinton began a bombing campaign that lasted for 78 days. He did this with no authorization from Congress. It is ironic that Congress impeached him, not for launching an illegal war, but for his part in the Monica Lewinsky affair! It is apparent that Congress has relinquished the role the Constitution assigned them.

Pat Buchanan has pointed out in his book *Where The Right Went Wrong* that nowhere has Congress' abdication of authority been more apparent or more complete than in the area of trade. In 1994, with only a *yes* or *no* vote permitted, Congress voted on the 23,000 page GATT Treaty to put the United States under the World Trade Organization. Under GATT, the U.S. has one vote. The European Union has 25, and their panels deliberate in secret. The WTO was given the power to authorize fines on the U.S, and to demand that the U.S. repeal American laws.

While President Clinton was lobbying for the passage of NAFTA, the Mexican peso was in trouble and seriously overvalued. But the American people were never told this. At that time we enjoyed a slight trade surplus with Mexico, and Clinton promised that this agreement would be of great benefit to both countries. Almost immediately after the passage of NAFTA, the weak peso threw Mexico into crisis. This was after the 1994 election, when Newt Gingrich championed the Contract With America in which the newly elected Republicans made certain promises to the American people.

During the lame duck session Clinton called for a meeting with Bob Dole and Newt Gingrich, a member of the CFR, to solve this crisis. They agreed that the United States would contribute $20 billion as part of an $80 billion international agreement to bail out Mexico. Gingrich sold out his Contract With America before his newly elected Republicans could even take office. The Mexican peso was devalued shortly thereafter, and our trade deficit with Mexico has swelled with large deficits ever since.

But this didn't bother Clinton at all. In fact, it seems that the ultimate purpose of NAFTA is to eventually eliminate the borders between the United States and Mexico, to create one economy and one nation of the Americas. This is another example of an American President putting his own secret political agenda ahead of the interests of the American people. This appears to be the first step to create a New World Government, under the United Nations.

While NAFTA was on its way toward passage, Mexican drug lords began buying up Mexican trucking companies, knowing that NAFTA meant easier access to the U.S. This would open up a huge new pipeline for them to smuggle their drugs into the States. Buchanan reports that Phil Jordan, intelligence chief of the DEA, reported this to President Clinton, who told Jordan to keep it quiet.

In his book *Unlimited Access*, Gary Aldrich describes the behavior of the Clinton staff during the years he served as an FBI Special Agent at the White House. Special Agent Aldrich had difficulty getting the Clinton staff to cooperate with him as he tried to conduct basic background checks, which he later figured out was due to the nefarious activities so many of them were involved in. It appears that much of the Clinton staff was or had been involved with drugs. One of Clinton's associates and friends was Little Rock businessman Dan Lasater, convicted of cocaine distribution, only to be pardoned by then-Governor Clinton.

We cannot afford to make other nations prosperous at our expense. Trade is not an end in itself, but a means to an end, which is to make America self-reliant. Alexander Hamilton was clear in wanting Congress to amend treaties negotiated by the Executive Branch. But the fast track provision completely surrendered this authority to the President. And though the Constitution gave Congress the power to coin money, this power had been transferred to the Federal Reserve. And now the IMF and the World Bank routinely put U.S. tax dollars at risk to bail out other countries' weak currencies, with billions of dollars coming directly out of the U.S. Treasury.

Congress has acted with complete disregard when it comes to the problem of immigration and our open borders. They wrote a law requiring employers to document the citizenship of their employees, but they wrote it so poorly that it has no teeth, making it impossible to enforce. 82 cases against employers came to trial in 1999, but in 2002 only 21 made it to court. Homeland Security requested $23 million to increase enforcement of our border security laws in 2003, but Congress approved only $5 million. Our Congress is made up mostly of lawyers. Could it be that they intentionally wrote this law to be unenforceable?

The Governor of Pennsylvania became so frustrated that he began to make arrests at the state level, but since illegal immigration is a federal offense, the prisoners were let off with a small fine in return for a promise to return for an immigration hearing at a later date. How many of them do you think showed up for that date?

This same tendency has also become quite clear when it comes to the Judiciary. For more than five decades, Congress has allowed the Judiciary to become a lawmaking body by failing to defend its unique right to legislate the law of the land. And the Supreme Court has been only too happy to fill the void and let their decisions assume the power of statute.

Congress has allowed its powers to be usurped by both the Executive and the Judiciary. They have become more concerned with fund raising and politically correctness, afraid they might lose their seat in Congress. Meanwhile, they make secret deals that provide billions of dollars in pork barrel spending each year. Though I know there are some strong and courageous people in Congress, far too many have been seduced by the power!

Congress has also abdicated its responsibility in another area: overseeing our involvement in the United Nations. The U.S. provides the U.N. seven billion dollars each year, over 22% of its annual budget. And what do we get for our money? U.N. representatives live here in relative luxury, while back home most of them would not be able to maintain the same status. They have come to view the U.S. Treasury as their own private piggy bank, and they raid it as often and for as much as they can.

Since its inception, the United Nations has represented an idealistic concept of what we thought the world should be: a free and democratic universe where all people are given the opportunity to succeed, to express and enjoy their freedom. But the truth of the matter is that the U.N. has become a cesspool of bureaucratic corruption and chaos.

Before invading Iraq, Bush went before the U.N. to plead his case and ask for their support, although they had failed to enforce any of the previous 14 resolutions to allow weapons inspectors back in. As Bob Woodward pointed out in his book, *Plan Of Attack*, Bush's primary concern with the pretense of asking for their permission was to provide cover for Don Rumsfeld and Tommy Franks as they put together the details of the Iraqi invasion.

The whole world would have been better off if Bush had decided to call the U.N. to task and challenged the very legitimacy of this irrelevant institution, instead of rushing off to war. Saddam stole $21 billion under the supervision of the United Nations, yet Kofi Annan refuses to open his books and reveal the secret deals. Paul Volker, who is investigating this scandal, has no power to subpoena the documents he needs. In all likelihood, money obtained through the Oil for Food program has been used to kill American soldiers in Iraq.

Many of our trading partners, including Russia, France, Germany, and China, had declared Saddam to be in violation of the U.N. resolutions. Had they stood up with us for what was right, we might have avoided going to war in Iraq. The list of Saddam's Oil for Food trading partners included several known contributors to terrorist organizations, and Bush knew Saddam had been skimming money off the top. And he certainly knew that France and Russia stood to lose billions of dollars in oil contracts if Saddam was removed.

The scandals that have plagued the United Nations under Kofi Annan are too numerous to mention, and some in Congress are calling for his resignation. For years now the U.N. has been redistributing our taxpayer dollars to third-world countries. Our budget deficits are strangling us, yet we give the U.N. the power to dictate what we Americans should be deciding here at home!

The U.N. has not only become irrelevant, it often works against the best interest of America. Now the U.N. wants to build a new 35-story headquarters in New York! My suggestion is to let one of the other nations of the world become home to this decayed institution. Since many people insist on its necessity, it will probably never disband, but that doesn't mean it can't be housed in another country.

Unless we are willing to surrender our autonomy, our liberty, and the American way of life to this degenerate institution, it is time to take a stand. It is time to tell this ineffective and ungrateful bureaucracy to move. Let's give then three years to find another country to take them in.

PART III

The coming of a world state is longed for by all the worst, and most distorted elements. This state, based on the principles of absolute equity of men, and a community of possessions, would banish all natural loyalties. In it no acknowledgment would be made of the authority of a father over his children, or of God over human society.

—Pope Benedict XV July 25, 1920

Political language is designed to make lies sound truthful and murder respectable.

—George Orwell

16

THE MEDIA IS THE MESSAGE

Anyone who has read Aldous Huxley's *Brave New World* can appreciate the irony of the title. Huxley wrote of a nightmare, an experiment in governmental control gone awry. It would appear that the alliance between the multinational corporations and our political parties is heading in that direction. One of the biggest offenders is MALDEF. The acronym stands for Mexican American Legal Defense and Education Fund.

On the surface, MALDEF appears to be fighting for the legal rights of Hispanics who are here illegally. Its three major objectives are: 1) helping illegal aliens get voting rights in American elections; 2) making the American taxpayers pay for the education of all illegal aliens; and 3) fighting to see that illegal aliens are entitled to get drivers' licenses in the U.S. It was Senator Pat Roberts who, along with Senator Rockefeller, made sure that the Intelligence Reform Bill of 2004 afforded illegal aliens the right to get American drivers' licenses. As stated earlier, Pat Roberts has received $300,000 from agribusiness over the last several years,

Unofficial polls conducted late in 2004 by CNN on *Lou Dobbs Tonight*, show that nearly 85% of Americans believe that illegal aliens should *not* have drivers licenses, and 95% of Americans believe that they should *not* be entitled to the constitutional rights afforded American citizens. Dobbs revealed that MALDEF is actually a front organization for large multinational corporations who favor Bush's open border policy. Coke Cola, McDonalds, Time Warner, and Tyson Foods are some of MALDEF's supporters.

It was MALDEF that caused California's proposition 187, which required welfare recipients to show proof of citizenship, to go down in defeat in the courts. They are now leading the charge against Proposition 200, a similar proposition that passed in Arizona in 2004. The Congress has stated that it will take up the immigration issue again in early 2005. If our politicians do not take action and stand up for the American people, our only alternative will be a national boycott of corporations supporting MALDEF.

Looking at another issue: how many people can remember the time when drug companies were not allowed to advertise on television? Why are they now allowed to come into our homes night after night and subtly seduce us into believing that there is a magic pill or a drug that can cure all our aches and pains? It has been widely acknowledged that our senior citizens are being over-medicated, yet we are bombarded with ads telling us to run to our doctor as soon as we feel the slightest ache or pain. The drug companies claim these ads help the consumer to be more informed about their health, making it easier for us to dialogue with our doctors. But the facts presented by Lou Dobbs in November 2004, tell another story.

The price of drugs to consumers went up 7.4% per year between 1993 and 2003. Drug company advertising is up 30% in the last 12 moths, to three billion dollars in 2004—they are now spending more on advertising than on research. Many patients now go to their doctors with a list of drugs they are interested in, rather than presenting their symptoms. The constant advertising is starting to cause people to doubt their health, even if they feel fine.

Some doctors have stated that this is creating a dangerous mindset, where the marketplace is dominating science. It is the drug companies that fund 80% of all medical research on drugs, and their results are five times more likely than unbiased studies to favor their pocketbooks. It is clear that the sole purpose of the FDA is the well being of the drug companies, not that of the American people. Former Congressman Billy Tauzin has recently been hired by PHARMA, a lobbyist for major drug companies. PHARMA will pay him well to make sure the drug companies continue to receive favorable legislation. And we can expect that the list of drugs taken off the market in the coming years due to faulty research will continue to grow. The FDA was set up by the drug companies to police themselves, to make it appear that they were working for the public's best interest, when just the opposite is true. This is exactly what the big bankers did in early 1900s to establish the Federal Reserve System.

In October, 2004, a CNN news segment dealt with the financial crisis in our health care system. It examined the latest technology, implanting patients just underneath the skin with a microchip containing their entire medical history. The reporter explained that this chip could save the life of an individual brought into the hospital in an emergency, for it would reveal allergies and other pertinent information that might be relevant.

Like guns and money, technology is inherently neither bad nor good. It all depends on how it is used. But they (the government? the insurance companies?) are already trying to sell us on these ideas. And if they can put our medical history on one of these chips, they could put our entire lives on one: our financial history, our voting record, what we read. This has the potential to be a huge invasion of our privacy, and the American people deserve a chance to discuss this technology before it is shoved down our throats under the guise of making us safer.

At the Hong Kong airport there are now electronic sensors that scan to check each potential passenger's temperature as they pass by, for they are worried about the SARS virus. Anyone with a fever is not allowed to fly for two days. The reason this is so important is that the next generation of nano-technology will be the size of dust particles. The federal government, along with such companies as IBM, HP, and Dupont, spent seven billion dollars in 2003 to perfect atmospheric tracking particles. These invisible chips will be able to track incredible amounts of data without your even knowing they have attached to you. If we don't start a dialogue now, we probably never will, and that could be very dangerous.

Our government has sponsored this alliance of multinational drug companies, doctors, and the media, and it appears that the real loser is the American people. But what does the government get out of this relationship? The answer is, a population that is becoming increasingly docile, that consumes painkillers and erectile dysfunction drugs for recreation and to escape the loneliness of a dysfunctional society.

According to a CNN survey in September, 2004, 36% of the public now gets all their news from TV, while 74% get some news from television. As a society, we are becoming more dependent on the government to tell us what is right and what is wrong, and the media companies have become the instruments of dissemination. Anyone who doubts this should take a look at Bernard Goldberg's two books, *Media Bias* and *Arrogance*.

Serious reporters were very upset when Dan Rather used forged evidence in an attempt to discredit Bush's military record. I think some of the media moguls were more concerned that this might cause the public to scrutinize the media's reporting of the news more closely. And then we might discover that the alliance between the media and the government does not have America's best interest at heart. As Marshall McCluen said, *the media is the message.*

For instance, CNN aired a program in November, 2004, and again in January, 2005, called *Immigrant Nation, Divided Nation*. Its focus was on the vast number of illegal aliens fast becoming a fixture in a small Atlanta town. The tone and attitude of the story were sympathetic to the plight of the illegal aliens. The reporter, a Latina herself, told how they had come here to make a better life. She spoke with several townspeople about the Mexican invasion, and interviewed some of the employers who had hired them. These employers proceeded to say that these were good people and good workers, and that they were happy to have them. Nobody is denying that they are good people. However, that does not excuse our government's failure to enforce our laws. Not a word was said about the higher profit margins the employers were making as they too broke the law. We then heard about a Mexican woman who had been diagnosed with cancer, and had run up $80,000 of medical expenses which the state paid for. Her husband was also ill and receiving free medical care.

There was another story about a woman who had left her two young children behind in Mexico. She was here illegally and had already tried to sneak her children across the border, but she had been caught. She stated defiantly that she was going to try again soon. Her attitude was that America was wrong for keeping her and her children apart.

CNN's whole point was to make us to sympathetic to the illegal aliens. CNN certainly could have interviewed some of the illegal aliens filling the jails in California for murder and rape, or given us some statistics about how much more it now costs taxpayers to run overcrowded schools and hospitals. But CNN had an agenda. Their parent, Time Warner, is a sponsor of MALDEF. These large companies don't really care that they are destroying America, as long as their bottom line shows a healthy profit.

CNN aired another special in November, 2004, called *Saudi Arabia: Kingdom On The Brink?* It started with Prince al Alaweed bin

Talal, a very wealthy man intent on changing the rigid customs of his country. Then, riding the elevator down from his office to a ground-floor mall, we find the religious police on patrol, making sure the women are properly dressed and that no one speaks out against the royal governing family.

At the heart of the issue is the fact that 1.3 billion Muslims bow five times a day in the direction of Mecca and Medina, both in Saudi Arabia. These two sites are considered most sacred, and many Muslims believe they have been defiled by the presence of Westerners who support the royal families. It is these few royal families that enjoy tremendous wealth, while not too far away their countrymen live in poverty and despair. It is in one such slum that the head of Paul Johnson was found, the American truck driver who was kidnapped by terrorists and then beheaded.

With 75% of the population under 27 years of age, the main question was: can the royal family institute change fast enough to settle the civil unrest of the population, or will the Saudi royal family be toppled by terrorists? We were shown several points of view, but we were left with some hope that the Saudi government would survive.

But it was the unstated message that was important. We were charmed and sympathetic to the young man who lived in the slums, and to the efforts of the royal family to change. And of course we were not sympathetic to the terrorists who fight this change. Since it is obvious that our economy is highly dependent on oil from Saudi Arabia, the unstated question is: will we be willing to fight to defend the royal family, should the terrorists try to overthrow them?

As I see it, this program was propaganda intended to win the support of the American people for our good friend Saudi Arabia. True, CNN did disclose at the beginning of the program that the wealthy Prince al Alaweed bin Talal is a major player in the American stock market—in fact, he owns a significant number of shares in Fox, which owns Fox

Broadcasting; in Disney, which owns ABC; and in Time Warner, which owns CNN. Should we be surprised? What would you expect the position of CNN to be when it comes to one of their large shareholders?

Are the American people being set up to go to war to defend Saudi Arabia in case of civil war? I would suggest that the U.S. military has already drawn up plans to defend Saudi Arabia in the event of a terrorist uprising. And bin Laden threw down the gauntlet with the release of his Internet video on December 17, 2004, in which he very clearly articulated that one of his primary goals is to bring down the Saudi government.

Early in the twentieth century there was another man who knew how to influence the media. His name was Willi Munzenberg, and he was a German Communist. Leon Trotsky had introduced Willi to Lenin as a *wunderkind* of sorts, and by 1921 he was the de facto director of the Soviet covert propaganda operation in the West. In *Double Lives*, Stephen Koch tells us that Willi was involved in the secret work of disseminating Soviet propaganda abroad. His work was profoundly influential and carried over to the reign of Stalin.

It must be noted here that the House of Rothschild bought the Reuters News Service in the late 1880s. Reuters supplies newspapers and magazines with the news on a worldwide basis. This was an asset to the Rothschilds in their move to dethrone the Russian royal family as payback for assisting Lincoln in America's civil war. It also gave Willi a powerful platform for his media campaign against the West. What is also interesting is that there is almost never a mention of either the Rockefellers or the Rothschilds in the media.

The objective was to cultivate the image of the Soviet Union as the liberator of humanity, the avenger of ancient evils, and the enforcer of a new heaven worldwide. As a master press agent, Willi's goal was to create an image in America and Europe of a humanitarian Soviet Union. Lenin wanted the Western world to believe that the foreign policy of the Soviet Union was based on the most essential elements of human decency. Willi's job was to instill an intrinsic feeling in Westerners that to challenge or criticize Soviet policy was the mark of a bad, bigoted, or stupid person, while support of these policies was an indication of forward-looking individuals of sensibility and refinement.

Willi developed *agents of influence*, spies who were trained at great length to get close to influential people of the West and employ any means available to shape their opinions. He invented ways of blurring the distinction between legal and illegal. He trained his operatives to target specific people, learn their likes and dislikes, and then manage to become a part of their lives. Agents like Kim Philby got their start in ostensibly legal occupations and then wormed their way into position, as did the so-called "Ladies of the Kremlin," who used their physical charms of seduction.

The goal was never to take over America by force, but to shape the opinions of important intellectuals around the world to be sympathetic to communism. Willi's targets included Lillian Hellman, Andre Malraux, Ernest Hemingway, Dorothy Parker, John Dos Passos, and Bertold Brecht, among others. Some, like Sinclair Lewis, fell in love with their agents and stayed with them until they died. Yet Willi stressed that they avoid at all costs ever using the name of the Communist Party. This was a plan of *secrecy and deniability*. If the target did not suspect that their friend/lover/wife was a Communist, then their expressions of support and sympathy for the principles of Communism would be heartfelt and real. They could loudly support the humanity of the Communist policies without ever being a Communist. This was part of Willi's genius.

Willi used all the tactics of manipulation, from group psychology to simple bribery. Always putting forth the face of humanity, moral righteousness, and idealism, he created a masterful sphere of influence that shaped world thinking. He placed bookstores near universities such as Columbia in New York, and started film societies on college campuses across America. His strategy was to take the moral claims of the adversary culture and make them appear to be part of the Communist philosophy. Willi would take the Negro issue in America, or middle class sexual repression, and show Stalinism embracing these repressed groups. Their ideals became his ideals. After defining the guilt of the offending culture, he would then offer the moral solution to the problem and ensnare his targets with the illusion of superiority and righteousness.

The net effect was to bind Stalinism to the self-evident truths of the downtrodden in the adversary culture. The effect was to show Stalin and his phony principles of liberation as an indispensable part of the enlightened life. Willi's targets believed in the ideals of a utopia that existed only in the Soviet Union, and they believed in them with an almost religious fervor; yet they retained the dignity of deniability.

Koch describes Willi's powers of influence as capable of producing committees of influence on important issues much as a magician pulls rabbits from a hat. He often used the name "Club of Innocents" when referring to his targets. After defining their guilt, he offered them not just innocence, but enlightened superiority, and they took to it by the millions.

Koch states that this paradigm was so successful that it survived his death and was quite instrumental in the peace movement in America during the Vietnam War, linking marches and committees on racial and sexual issues together. Willie had learned how to unlock the power of the media, and he used it to influence the free world in a way never before imagined. He was instrumental in putting a humanitarian face onto the most nightmarish evil, and yet made his innocent victims feel good in the roles they served.

Today, the power of the media is such a part of our psyche that we no longer question its viewpoint. We tend to swallow the syrup pumped into us each day without critically examining the messenger. It is up to us to demand more of our leaders and politicians, to educate ourselves, and to take an active role in government. We can no longer blindly trust them to get it right. The clarity of their wisdom is severely in doubt.

17

THE ROAD TO FREEDOM

In his forward to F. A. Hayek's book *The Road to Serfdom*, John Chamberlain says that full employment, social security, and freedom from want cannot be had unless they come as the by-products of a system that releases the free energies of individuals. When the government dictates that "the greatest good for the greatest number" becomes the law of the land, then the planners of the state have taken over. When this happens the creative ingenuity of the individual is suffocated, and free enterprise dies. The state then becomes dictator, and dictators always lead to less freedom.

America has survived and prospered because it was founded on the basis of individual liberty. Recall Maybury's claim that the more the laws of a nation reflect the principles of 1) doing all you have agreed to do and 2) not encroaching on others or their property, the more prosperous that society will be. That is a difficult standard to live up to, for an individual or a nation, but it is important that we strive to become a little better each and every day.

I recently read a book by John Perkins, *Confessions Of An Economic Hit Man*. In it he details his activity on behalf of large multinational corporations who hired him to swindle small countries out of their natural resources. John would make these countries large loans, and larger promises of wealth and prestige. But when they eventually could not make the payments on the debt, the multinationals would take their natural resources as payment. Their tactics started with negotiation and degenerated from there to more severe measures. He said that if all else failed, men from the Black Ops division would take over to insure success.

Perkins eventually discovered what was happening and left this business. He is now an advocate for the peoples of the world, opposing the multinationals he used to work for. He supports a more equitable distribution of wealth, and believes the world is entitled to the same rights and protections as are guaranteed to American citizens by our Constitution. But liberty can only exist where the people are willing to fight for it, as there will always be those with evil in their hearts who want to take it away.

Also, Perkins does not realize that the multinationals he worked for 30 years ago have changed their disguise. They now appear in the form of organizations like MALDEF, supporting the elimination of borders and the expansion of American liberties to the rest of the world. This is a utopian fantasy that is totally out of touch with reality—it is part of the propaganda. Under the guise of globalization, the same multinational forces are working behind the scenes to push America into a New World Order. This will make it easier for them to increase both their wealth and their power.

Bribery has been commonplace throughout the world since the beginning of commerce. In the United States, the multinationals hedge their bets by making campaign contributions to both parties. Should the New World Order become a reality, you can be sure that the multinational corporations will have even more leeway to enhance their profits with cheap labor and a centralized bureaucracy to accept their "contributions."

Mr. Perkins' San Francisco publisher, Barrett Koehler, at www. bkconnection.com, claims they are dedicated to a more equitable distribution of the world's wealth and resources. The links available at their web site make this very clear. However, I have a sneaking suspicion there is more going on here than meets the eye. If one were to dig deep enough, it might be discovered that some of the groups promising a utopian fantasy have motives that are not at all altruistic.

As Christmas approached in 2004, I heard Michael Douglas speaking in a TV ad on behalf of the United Nations, trying to raise funds for their efforts to fight AIDS around the world. This is an admirable effort, and it was kind of Mr. Douglas to give so generously. But how much of the money he raises will actually reach those in need, and how much will line the pockets of bureaucrats along the way? We are only just beginning to discover how deep the corruption went at the U.N. in the Oil For Food scandal. And there are so many more examples.

The U.N. does not appear to be very efficient at distributing humanitarian aid. One source, Mike Shanahan, seems to suggest that only 30 cents of every dollar reaches its intended source (www.SciDev. net) . That figure does not take into account any fraud or corruption.

Some people may think it unpatriotic to question the paradigm of government-funded aid packages. But there are a number of good reasons for doing so. One of them is an ethical dilemma. Government aid, whether it be direct or through quasi-governmental entities such as the World Bank, can only exist at the expense of private citizens. This is money taken by means of taxation that may go to causes not supported by most Americans; or it may come in the form of taxpayer-backed loans handed out to risky and oppressive regimes at lower rates that undercut competitors in the free market. In either case, personal liberty is decreased.

Private charity performs better than government charity for numerous reasons. First, there is less chance that the funds will be given to corrupt or inefficient groups in exchange for political favors to be returned at a later date. Second, the personal connection at the heart of many private charities cannot be duplicated by a governmental agency. Such a contribution will usually mean that more care is given to see that the aid goes to the people most in need, whereas a bureaucratic agency may be more concerned with simply getting the job done so its agents can go home. Private charity embodies the spirit of neighbor helping neighbor, which often leads to the current receiver later helping another group in a time of need. This kind of effort is not easily duplicated by government.

On the morning of January 10, 2005, Jefferies & Company, a large brokerage firm on Wall Street, announced that they would donate all of their profits from that day to the Tsunami relief effort for the Indonesian people. This included all of their income from commissions as well as their trading profits. On that same day, Price Waterhouse declared that they would oversee the proper distribution of the Tsunami relief aid, making sure that the process was efficient and that all of the supplies went to the proper destination. They did this because the United Nations can no longer be trusted.

The American people are the most generous people in the world. We do not need the U.N. to act as a parasitic middleman. The United Nations is a breeding ground for corruption, waste and mismanagement. Our determination to avoid unnecessary wars would render it obsolete. The American people need to get involved in helping America, especially those who have benefited the most by living here. In 2003 the number of new billionaires rose from 262 to 313; that is a 19% increase. We need their time and energy to champion the causes of education and poverty here at home. Their personal skills and involvement are just as important as their money, for they know how to get results. We need all Americans to step up and take the lead in solving the serious challenges that face us in the 21st century.

I was reading recently about some of the charities supported and sponsored by many of our film stars and athletes. Ben Affleck, David Arquette, Jeff Bridges, Kevin Bacon, Paul Newman, Robin Williams, Whoopi Goldberg, Elizabeth Taylor, and Mary Tyler Moore have raised many millions of dollars for such causes as cancer, AIDS, and diabetes. I could easily fill several pages naming film, TV, and sports celebrities who have given generously of themselves for worthy causes. They are doing this to give back to the country that has meant so much to them, and we need their help now more than ever.

A big part of what has made America great has been people of character and ingenuity helping out others less fortunate. Why couldn't Michael Fox and others who wish to support stem cell research join together and sponsor TV fund-raisers or music concerts, as Jerry Lewis has done for decades? I support stem cell research, but I do not believe that it is the duty of the government to provide it when we are so much in debt. Does everyone have the right to live to 100? I don't know. But I do know that we cannot continue to demand that our government try and fix every illness or problem that confronts us.

After the 2004 election, I watched Russell Simmons on a news program. He was very dedicated to getting out the youth vote, and he spoke about living with more love in our hearts. I completely agree with him that this is something that all of us need to work on. I don't know how to measure love, but with all of our technological innovations we may eventually come up with an instrument able to do just that. In the meantime, I think our only alternative is to measure our ability to become more responsible for ourselves and less dependent on government welfare. Maybe right now that is the highest form of love. The government should be here to preserve our liberties, prosecute criminals, and protect the homeland. Our Founding Fathers did not intend for us to be a welfare-warfare state.

There are many very poor and very ill people in America who need help. But if we try to provide for everyone, we will not be able to help anyone. We need people out there like Russell Simmons and Reverend Run to preach the *gospel of self-responsibility*. This is what Bill Cosby, an American hero, is doing. This is the spirit that, if followed, can unite America once again.

It is my belief that if the U.N. were eliminated, private American groups would get involved, and a much larger percentage of the funds raised would reach the people who need help. And Mr. Douglas would probably be just as generous with his time and support. The U.N. was set up by a group of people who were and are intent on ruling the world, although the U.N. bureaucracy is probably unaware of this fact, as are most Americans. The Global Elite has been very busy behind the scenes for many decades, patiently waiting for the time when their chosen representatives will be able to step in and run the show. I know that many will scoff at this idea, but in the following chapters I hope you will carefully consider the case I present.

18

THE ROOTS OF JIHAD

In 570 A.D. Mohammad founded Islam, which means *submission to God's Law*. By 630 it had achieved its own golden age. At its peak, the Muslim empire was actually far greater than even the Roman Empire. Often using the sword, it made new converts as it spread from Spain to Persia. Towns that surrendered without a fight were often offered lowered taxes, and many towns and villages accepted such an offer. While Europe was mired in the Dark Ages, a new wave of science and technology was booming under the Muslims. Our numbering system, the navigational instruments used by Columbus, surgery, anesthesia, pharmacology, and medical schools are just some of the advancements they were responsible for, according to Rose Wilder Lane in her book *From the Discovery of Freedom*. Their ideas eventually spread to Europe and helped start the Renaissance.

Pope Sylvester II, who lived from 940 to 1003, didn't like the fact that the Muslims were in control of the Holy Land, and he laid the groundwork for the Crusades, which began in 1093. Pope Urban promised the Crusaders that if they would wage war to take back the Holy Land, then all of their sins would be forgiven. They raped, murdered, and plundered as they made their way through Europe. By the time they reached the Holy Land, they were as bloodthirsty and brutal as any army that had come before them.

For two hundred years the death and destruction continued, in some of the most savage butchery mankind has ever seen. The Crusades didn't end, but rather they evolved into the Spanish Inquisition, in which more than three million Muslims and Jews were condemned and 300,000 were burned at the stake. The Catholics devised ingenious methods of torture, excruciating and barbarous. When Napoleon arrived and put a stop to it in 1808, the French soldiers, who were used to cruelty and bloodshed, could not stomach the sight of the naked and insane prisoners they found.

It was the Crusades that set the backdrop for much of the fighting that continues in the Middle East today. Animosity and personal grudges are passed down from generation to generation, becoming ever more bitter with the passing decades. When hatred is mixed with religion, it becomes a most poisonous and deadly brew.

As the Europeans began to colonize the world, they competed with each other to carve up the Middle East, creating boundaries that had previously never existed. The British took Egypt and Iraq and divided Iran with Russia, while the French took Lebanon and Syria and divided Morocco with Spain. The Middle East remains to this day mostly tribal communities, with individual loyalties belonging to their family, village, and friends. The people resent these borders and those who created them, much as we would resent another country coming to America and restructuring our borders.

In his book *The Thousand Year War in the Mideast*, Richard Maybury explains how the Europeans controlled their colonies. They selected the most vicious tribe in each area and supplied them with the money and weapons to subdue the other tribes. Mass torture and murder became commonplace, and still exist today. What the Europeans created were gangsters to do their killing for them. The name of Saudi Arabia came into existence because it was the tribe of Saud that the British selected to conquer the other four tribes in the area. To this day, the royal family is so afraid of its people that it maintains two armies of equal size so that if one army revolts, the other can be used against it.

Most of the Middle East is comprised of countries that have no freedom of speech, press, or religion. There are generally no elections or constitutions. One might even be tempted to call the ruling regimes fascists. There are about 10 million Arab "haves" and 250 million Arab "have-nots."

Our Founding Fathers were adamant that we not get involved in European politics, that we should go to war only to defend ourselves. They believed in the *doctrine of neutrality*, though they were not always able to practice it themselves.

In the early nineteenth century there were many Muslims living in the states of North Africa who claimed the right to control the Gulf of Sidra, off the coast of Tripoli, Libya. The Muslims still bore a grudge from the Crusades and the Inquisition, and taxed European ships that sailed along the African coast. And they raised these taxes rather frequently. The European merchants convinced their government to pay these taxes, but the small and struggling American government could no longer afford this cost.

In 1801, the Pasha of Tripoli captured an American merchant trying to escape the tax and imprisoned the sailors. The U.S. government sent the Navy and the Marines to attack the Muslims, which in the long run was much more expensive than paying the tax would have been. Thus began our first, but not our last, entry into world politics to protect American interests. The Barbary Wars, as they were called, began under President Jefferson and ended in 1815. These wars set the historical precedent for using our military to protect the ever expanding interests of the business community as it spread all over the globe. Protecting these interests would become the cornerstone for much future aggression and war.

It was once thought that World War II would be the war to end all wars. We now know that that was a naive idea. We must therefore acknowledge two indisputable facts: first, that the nature of man is such that there will always be some kind of aggressive conflict going on in the world; and second, that it is in the nature of man to seek power, to become obsessed with power, to become addicted to power.

This begs the question, how can we deal with a brutal world that will never change? It has been said that one definition of insanity is to keep doing the same thing over and over again, expecting a different result. Obviously, the first thing we must do is to readjust our attitudes and expectations. We have to accept that the world will never be a utopia, and that efforts to that end are doomed to failure. The world will always be a hurtful and dangerous place. This is a fact of life.

In the next chapter I will review our history of warfare in the Middle East and then begin to examine the real sources power in Washington D.C.

19

WAR IS POLITICS CARRIED OUT BY OTHER MEANS

In 1953 the U.S. government helped to install the Shah as the leader of Iran. As our good friend in the region, this murderous dictator held power until January of 1979, when the Ayatollah Khomeini overthrew him and created a Western-style republic based on Islamic law. In November, 1979, he seized the American embassy in Teheran and took the employees hostage. This was extremely damaging to the American psyche, and caused President Carter to freeze all Iranian assets in the U.S. This in turn created a financial panic, for many other countries worried that we might freeze their assets as well. Our interest rates went through the roof, hitting record highs.

Then in December of 1979 the Soviets invaded Afghanistan, and the U.S. government feared they would break through to the Persian Gulf and seize the Saudi oil fields. Fearing for their survival, the Saudis agreed to finance a guerrilla war against the Soviets in Afghanistan. President Carter ordered the CIA to recruit, organize, and supply the indigenous forces that had already begun to resist the Soviets. Fortified with Saudi money, the U.S. government was, for the first time, able to turn the tables on the Soviets and foment a successful guerrilla war against them.

Long a country of feuding warlords, Afghanistan was one of the few countries that had succeeded in thwarting the invasion attempts of Alexander the Great and the British Empire. Given that Islam was the only unifying theme available to the U.S. to instigate resistance against the Soviets, we formed an alliance with a faction of radical Afghan Muslims. The Pakistanis, who also had a large Muslim population, joined in the alliance and provided an intelligence network through their ISI.

The Saudis decided not to finance this operation with government funds, but instead tapped private resources from wealthy families like the bin Ladens. When Reagan was elected President he put William Casey in charge of the CIA, and Casey saw the opportunity to bring together Muslims from many different Islamic countries. Once hardened into a tough fighting unit fueled by their religious bonds, the radical Muslim framework became the basis for resistance against the Soviets.

The U.S. government and the Saudis had another parallel interest: containing Iran, which is primarily Shiite. The Shiites are quite different from the Saudi, who are Wahabi, a very conservative strand of Sunni Islam. The U.S. had supported the Shah of Iran in his war against Iraq in the 1970s. Now, however, the U.S. decided to turn the tables and support Iraq against Iran. The U.S. government did not believe Iraq could defeat Iran, but hoped they would engage Iran in a long, drawn-out war that would leave them both depleted.

The Saudis and other Persian Gulf sheiks were willing to finance this war between Iran and Iraq, but Saddam Hussein needed more motivation. He wanted to be the dominant power in the Persian Gulf, and he wanted to reclaim Kuwait, historically part of Iraq until the British Empire separated it off to assure their access to oil. The U.S. government quietly assured Saddam that once he had defeated Iran, we would not stand in his way of reclaiming Kuwait as his prize.

So now the U.S. was involved in two wars in the Middle East at the same time. Most of the money to finance the wars was coming from the Saudis, with U.S. companies selling the missiles and munitions. At the same time, the CIA was teaching the Muslim radicals in Afghanistan how to wage covert warfare.

When the radical Muslims defeated the Soviet Union it was of crucial importance, for it was the first Islamic victory over a non-Islamic force in centuries, and a superpower to boot. The Islamic world had been occupied by the French as well as the British, and had also been crushed by the Israelis in several wars. Even the U.S. had beaten them in the Barbary Wars. However, after the radical Muslims' victory over the Soviet Union, the recruiting network and the financial arrangements remained in place, even though the U.S. government quickly lost interest.

In his book *America's Secret War,* George Friedman points out that the Afghan fighters were some of the best and brightest soldiers ever fielded in the Middle East. But the governments, including Saudi Arabia, didn't want these holy warriors back home where they could cause trouble. So the best of them, several thousand, were left stranded in a foreign country.

The U.S. government was still busy, doing everything it could to make sure Iraq would not be able to win the war against Iran. The U.S. shifted its weight back and forth, supplying missiles and other supplies to Iran. The war dragged on for 10 years and cost millions of lives. Iraq finally won by default, when Iran was too exhausted to fight anymore.

On July 25, 1990, Saddam informed U.S. Ambassador April Glaspie that he was going to claim his prize and invade Kuwait. Uninformed of a policy change, Glaspie informed Saddam that the U.S. had no opinion on such border disputes. In August he invaded Kuwait, which caused the U.S. to send troops into Saudi Arabia for Operation Desert Storm. This angered radical Muslims as well as the religious Wahabi, for Saudi Arabia is home to the holy cities of Mecca and Medina, the birthplace of Islam.

The skilled Muslim fighters that had defeated the Soviets were outraged at the presence of U.S. troops on the holy ground of Islam. And now they were practiced in the CIA tactics of covert warfare. Centuries of grievance against the British, the French, the Dutch, and now the Americans gave rise to a plan to revive the glory of the Islamic world that went back to the Crusades. Bin Laden intended a war of righteous and holy indignation against the infidel, the Christian United States, the dominant global superpower. The U.S. had inserted and protected murderous dictators to keep the oil flowing. Bin Laden's objective was to convince the Islamic world that they were under attack by the major religions of the world, including the Christians, Jews, and Hindus.

Friedman details the thoroughness and patience of al Qaeda in its planning of September 11. He illustrates where and why the U.S. intelligence was weak, and what al Qaeda did to exploit these deficiencies. Bin Laden used each attack to determine our weakness and estimate our government's response time. His cunning use of propaganda, passion, and religious fervor ignited the radical Muslims. The appeal was simple but effective, an all-out campaign of revenge. Michael Scheuer warns us in his book, *Imperial Hubris*, not to dismiss the patience or the intelligence of bin Laden, for he is well equipped to carry out his objectives.

But the real question is, have we learned any lessons from history? All the great nations of the past have crumbled, and *imperial hubris* has always been a factor in their demise. What is imperial hubris? I would define it as the belief that one's own nation is superior to all other nations, that it is somehow preordained by the Almighty to enforce its will and domination upon the rest of the world. The following statement by Madeleine Albright is a statement of imperial hubris: "*If we have to use force, it is because we are America. We are the indispensable nation. We stand tall. We see further into the future.*"

Albright's attitude is dangerous; it is a doorway to destruction. Our dead and wounded American soldiers and their families have paid a terrible price. We have to start being honest, acknowledging that we are and have been fighting in the Middle East because their oil is vital to our economy. Unless we admit this, then we are simply lying to ourselves. We have used our military to secure cheap oil, and all the statements about making the world safe for democracy are false. Had we started to develop alternative fuel sources back in 1973, after the first oil embargo, we would have never had to suffer the effects of September 11. True, it would have been expensive, but we would be ahead of the curve right now instead of wasting all of our resources, not to mention our brave young soldiers, fighting a war that cannot be won as we begin to focus on Iran.

Unfortunately, it is the enemy within that has been pulling the strings, dictating a foreign policy of death and destruction that causes us to be hated around the world. This enemy is an evil force with a messianic plan: to establish a New World Order. This was its goal throughout the twentieth century and they have only grown stronger so far in this century. The American people want peace. *But the shadow government controls our leaders and maneuvers constantly behind our backs for world domination.*

The real power in our universe is wielded by a small elite group of men that hide behind what appears to be an altruistic organization of world peace. The Council on Foreign Relations (CFR) is a nonprofit organization dedicated to the understanding of U.S. foreign policy and international affairs through the exchange of ideas. So says its Annual Report. It includes presidents, ambassadors, members of the Pentagon, NATO, wealthy industrialists, Supreme Court justices, congressmen, federal judges, the media, etc. They hold open meetings and publish membership lists.

The 1999 CFR Annual Report states three goals: 1) Add value by improving understanding of world affairs and by providing new ideas for U.S. foreign policy; 2) Transform the Council into a truly international organization to benefit from the expertise and experience of leaders worldwide; and 3) Find and nurture the next generation of foreign policy leaders and thinkers.

On the surface it all seems so harmless, so wonderfully global, that few Americans would suspect it as a front for the most diabolical secret organization the world has ever known. We expect monsters to look like Lenin and sound like Stalin or Hitler. But what we are dealing with here is an incredibly sophisticated group of individuals, linked with some of the most important people in the world to give it credibility and a shield of invisibility.

The circle of influence in this group begins on the edges, with many well known names from the media: Barbara Walters, Dan Rather, Peter Jennings, Ed Bradley, Garrick Utley, Marvin Kalb, Frank Sesno, Robin Wright, John Chancellor, Paula Zahn, and Tom Brokaw all are CFR members. The list goes on, with some, such as George Stephanopolos, belonging to other shadow groups as well.

In the second circle are the wealthy industrialists who own the large multinationals, and within that circle is the smaller group of presidents and heads of state, including Presidents Bush one and two, Bill Clinton, and Senator Kerry. The innermost circle is probably not even known but to a very select few, for they are the Puppet Masters, the ones who pull the strings that make the nations dance.

In his book *Who's Who of the Elite*, Robert Gaylon Ross points out that there are 20 different places in the 1992 CFR Annual Report that tell the members they had better keep secret the matters discussed in council meetings. Ross gives the actual language and the page numbers of these demands for secrecy.

In his book *The Anglo-American Establishment*, Carroll Quigley describes how three very wealthy men—Cecil Rhodes, William Snead, and Reginald Brett—put the wheels into motion that formed the secret Round Table Groups set up in seven different countries between 1910 and 1915. These secret societies evolved into the Institutes for International Affairs and the Council on Foreign Relations in 1920. Their goal is nothing less than establishing one global empire controlled by the Global Elite.

In 1954, a sister organization named The Bilderbergs (BB) was formed, named after the Bilderberg Hotel, where they had their first meeting. This is the most secretive of the three sister organizations, which also include the Trilateral Commission. The Bilderberg membership is made up of kings and queens, presidents and prime ministers, as well as the media elite, including Leslie Stahl, and Bill Moyers. Mort Zuckerman is part of a rare breed, for he belongs to all three of these organizations (which I refer to as the Elite Three).

BB requires that the resorts where annual meetings are held be cleared out 48 hours before their arrival. They then debug the entire grounds and import their own staff of cooks, waiters, etc. The host government is reimbursed for providing extensive security precautions. Ross states that the CIA helped organize and sponsor the formation of this group, and he believes they are still involved to this day.

Zbigniew Brezinsky put the Trilateral Commission (TC) together, at the request of David Rockefeller in 1973. It includes members from Europe, North America, and Japan. In his book *With No Apologies*, Senator Goldwater describes the TC as David Rockefeller's newest international cabal, intended to be the vehicle for multinational consolidation of the commercial and banking interests by seizing control of the United States government.

Ross states that it was this Global Elite who put Jimmy Carter in the White House and made sure that Senator Goldwater failed in his attempt to become President. It appears that David Rockefeller may be the Global Czar, for he has been head of all three groups at one time and may still be to this day. To these organizations the lives, liberty, and future of the American people are no more than cannon fodder for those who would continue with their policy of global wars and social engineering.

Speculation has it that the power behind these three organizations is the Rockefellers, with an estimated fortune of more than $11 trillion, and the Rothschilds, whose wealth may well exceed $100 trillion.

If we are going to escape the manifest destiny of the Global Elite, we must divorce ourselves from the partisan bickering of the Left and the Right. We must educate our families, and ourselves and stop accepting the condensed version of the Republican/Democratic sound bites. The ability of these secret groups to control every aspect our government is devastating. They have distracted us with political infighting and arguing to such an extent that we have lost sight of the truth: We are in this together, for we are all Americans. We cannot continue to let the power junkies and the political addicts keep us at each other's throats, or we will fall, a house divided.

20

THE CAUSE OF SEPTEMBER 11

Sometimes the truth is right in front of us and we still don't recognize it. Anyone who believes that September 11 occurred because America loves freedom and democracy should go stand on their head in a corner somewhere. The terrorists hate us for what we have done, not what we believe! The words of bin Laden in the video he released just prior to our 2004 national election tell the story:

"For every dollar that I spent on September 11, America has spent a million. We are going to bleed America dry, until they are no longer a superpower."

He told us very clearly what he was doing. He baited us into what has every chance of becoming a world war against 1.3 billion Muslims. Are we going to spend the next 50 years trying to democratize an entire region that has never in its history had a democracy? It would be less expensive, in terms of lives and money, to pay a little more at the gas pump until we can come up with an alternative fuel source. The creativity and ingenuity of America is limitless; surely this is a goal we can achieve. Why are we chasing windmills in the desert? Is this the Global Elite's way of bankrupting America?

Where in our Constitution does it say that our mission is to spread freedom and democracy? Our Founding Fathers knew such a task was impossible!

If we were to pull out of the Middle East today, would radical Muslims still try to terrorize us? Maybe. But it's more likely they would be too busy fighting amongst themselves to try and attack the U.S. Then we could spend the hundreds of billions of dollars we would have wasted in the Middle East on making America stronger from within, by securing our borders and documenting the illegal aliens already here. America is stretched far too thin to even think about extending the war in Iraq to Iran or Syria. But the Bush administration is doing just that!

The National Guard makes up 40% of our troops in Iraq, and already there have been more deaths in the Guard than in all of Vietnam. We need them home. We need to be training them to do what the Constitution intended: protect the homeland. We need to upgrade their equipment and defenses. The neoconservative policy calls for a permanent military presence on six continents so that the U.S. government can police the entire world. This is playing right into the hands of the fanatic Muslims. It is an idea that will bankrupt America and kill many of our innocent young sons and daughters.

On his TV show *The Factor*, Bill O'Reilly has asked several guests why someone doesn't drop a dime on Musab al Zarqawi for the $25 million reward. He can't believe that none of the radicals want the reward. Obviously, the people fighting us in Iraq are fighting for something they value much more than money. As George Friedman points out in *America's Secret War*, they are fighting to dethrone the dictators that govern the region and the Americans that have empowered them for so long. It is their homeland, and they have shown themselves to be hardened fighters and extremely patient.

Everybody agrees that Hitler was mad, but he understood enough about people and politics to convince a lot of people to follow him. And Saddam Hussein is probably just as mad, intoxicated with his own delusions of power. But when he declared in 1991, as the U.S. prepared to attack him, that the upcoming battle would be the "mother of all wars," perhaps he understood something about the psyche of the Muslim people that only an insider could understand. Maybe he realized that the hatred and animosity of the Muslim people for the West was beyond anything we could comprehend. The British and French had divided Syria, Lebanon, Palestine, and Iraq for the oil. The U.S. had empowered the Shah of Iran for 25 years so that he could butcher and terrorize his own people while looting the oil profits. Maybe Saddam understood something we could not, because of our hubris.

At the end of World War II a group of Jews, desperate and utterly demoralized, were looking for a home of their own. Many of these Jews emigrated from Europe to Palestine, presumably unaware that 10 centuries of hatred and hostility still separated the Muslims from the Europeans. Two of the most persecuted peoples on the planet, they probably would have solved their problems and found a way to live together had they been left alone to work it out.

Evan Elband, Director of the Center On Peace And Liberty, points out that from 1949 to 1970 the U.S. government gave Israel little financial support, yet in the 1967 War Israel managed to smash several Arab enemies at once. After 1971, when our military aid to Israel went up more than 20-fold, their military actually deteriorated, as evidenced in the Middle East Wars of 1973 and 1982. Elband believes that if the U.S. stopped all aid to Israel, which currently accounts for only three percent of their GDP, they would change their policies and more easily resolve their disputes with the Palestinians.

Friedman believes the failure of the U.S. strategy in the 1990s was a failure to recognize that *there is no such thing as a neutral intervention.* Every intervention, no matter what the rhetoric proclaims, will favor one country and hurt another. And that includes foreign aid! The bottom line will always be more enemies.

The history of our actions in the Middle East complicated and exacerbated the problems of this region right from the start. Our dependence on oil has been at the root of our involvement in the area. If we were to adopt a position of neutrality and pull back from our involvement there, we would have to pay more for our oil, to be sure. But like all other commodities, the price of oil will eventually seek a natural balance of supply and demand. And at least we would stop making things worse. Our Founding Fathers admonished us to engage in commerce but to stay out of other countries' politics. Their reasoning should be very clear by now.

On November 14, 2004, Mike Scheuer, author of *Imperial Hubris*, came out of the shadows to appear on *60 Minutes*. A former CIA analyst, he was critical of the CIA's Middle East policies and the U.S. position on the war on terror. He left the CIA and revealed his identity because he felt there was a high probability that al Qaeda would strike us with a nuclear bomb of some kind in the not-too-distant future. He also said that we must consider all our options, even our relationship with Israel, which he described as being akin to "the tail wagging the dog."

I recently came across this story from the periodical *Forward*, the oldest Jewish magazine in America. On March 15, 2002, staff writer Marc Perelman wrote a story of five Israelis arrested in New Jersey on 9/11. All five worked for Urban Moving Systems, a company with few discernible assets. The Israeli owner fled to Israel immediately after the arrests. The five Israelis were held for more than two months and subjected to an unusual number of polygraph tests. When two of their names showed up on a CIA/FBI database of foreign intelligence operatives, the FBI's counterintelligence division took charge. When this division handles a case, it is extremely serious and kept very secret.

The Israelis were held in solitary confinement until mid-October of 2001 at the high-security Metropolitan Detention Center in Brooklyn. According to one high-ranking American intelligence officer, who asked not to be named, the FBI concluded that they were conducting a Mossad surveillance operation, and that Urban Moving Systems of NJ was a front. Both governments denied any allegations of spying, and the five Israelis pled guilty to visa violations and were deported back to Israel at the end of November 2002.

At about the same time, Carl Cameron of Fox News reported that more than 60 Israelis had been taken into custody after 9/11. Other reports suggest that there were as many as 160 Israelis in the U.S., many posing as art students, and there was an uncanny correlation between the 40 cities where they stayed and the locations of the 9/11 terrorists. One of them had lived next door to Mohammad Atta for a while prior to 9/11. The hint was that some of these agents had been spying for Israel and had become aware of the terrorist plans, but had only provided the FBI with vague suggestions as to what might be in the works.

Fox news did not reveal any specifics, claiming that the information was classified. Rupert Murdoch, the owner of Fox News, was a prominent supporter of President Bush's invasion of Iraq. There are certainly no hard facts to prove that Israel had discovered the intent of the terrorists prior to 9/11 and failed to warn us. But it would have been logical for them to assume that after such an attack the U.S. would become more aggressive in the affairs of the Middle East, to the benefit of Israel. A co-worker of the five employees at Urban Moving Systems is reported to have said they were laughing and joking on the day the World Trade Center was bombed.

One would have to assume that Bush became aware of these facts after 9/11, but did not want this information released to the public. The neoconservatives are all about fighting for Israel. As soon as the U.S. invaded Afghanistan, Israel began to attack the Palestinians very aggressively. Ariel Sharon appeared repeatedly on the nightly news to defend the Israeli attacks, claiming that he was only doing what the United States was doing: protecting itself from terrorists.

It has been postulated that had the United States not entered either world war, the history of the world would have turned out quite differently. Had we not entered World War I, the French would not have been able to force the Treaty of Versailles on the German people. Would more people have died? I don't know, but we did lose 116,000 American soldiers in that war. Had World War I ended in a draw, Germany would not have been so devastated , and Hitler would not have been able to fill the minds of the German people with thoughts of hatred, anger, and revenge.

Had we not entered World War II, would Hitler and Stalin have ended up killing each other? I don't know. Maybe. Would the winner have emerged very strong? Probably not, for the war would have taken a major toll on both sides. Had we stayed out of the war, would we have ended up dropping two atomic bombs on Japan to impress Stalin? I don't think so. I have no doubt that FDR goaded the Japanese into an unnecessary war and sacrificed Pearl Harbor in the process. Would we have then spent almost a half-century fighting a Cold War with the Soviet Union? Would we have gone to war with Vietnam?

The President is standing firm, committed to fight until we have secured a democratic state in Iraq. Our odds of victory are slim, for the insurgents are fighting a guerrilla war to avenge Western domination that has spanned most of the last century. One fact that argues against our victory is that the Iraqi police have not shown the hardened warrior spirit that al Zarqawi seems to possess. Quite often they will simply leave their post when attacked. The Iraqi will to fight has not yet been proven, especially when their families are threatened and butchered by insurgents if they ignore warnings to stop supporting the U.S.

William Lind pointed out in the November, 2004 issue of *The American Conservative* that a defensive war is usually easier to win than an offensive war. He quoted Carl von Clausewitz, who stated that defensive warfare is intrinsically stronger than an offensive war. This is especially true when the enemy is fighting a guerrilla war, when he has nowhere to go and is not constrained by any rules of war, such as the

Geneva Convention. Muslim insurgents seem willing to sacrifice almost any number of fighters to win. Our incredibly brave and courageous soldiers are fighting an enemy where even a child can be a combatant.

Another issue is the cost of fighting this war. On November 11, 2004, the NY Times told the story of a single sniper in Fallujah who kept 150 U.S. Marines and their supporting aircraft, tanks, and artillery tied down for nine hours. He eventually escaped to fight another day. The point is that the sniper spent about $10 in ammunition for an inexpensive gun, while the operation probably cost us hundreds of thousands of dollars. This is being played out again and again in Iraq, and it doesn't take into account the cost in human lives when a cheap car bomb kills eight or 10 of our soldiers.

The imperial hubris of the U.S. government could very well be our downfall. But it may not be too late. If we can change the way we behave toward the rest of the world, there is a great possibility we can survive and prosper. But we will have to reign in our politicians and their egomaniacal drive for power. And we will have to clip the wings of the Global Elite. If someone attacks us, we have every right to annihilate them. If we fail to capture or kill their leaders, as we have with bin Laden, we can coordinate with other nations to hunt them down like dogs. Our friends around the world will assist us in this because it is in their best interest. But our effort to democratize the Middle East is insanity.

A strong military with an all-volunteer army is essential. But we cannot afford to police the rest of the world. Why are we defending Europe against an enemy that disappeared 15 years ago? Why do we have troops in 144 countries today? We need to fortify this country, our borders, and so much more. The Global Elite has deluded us into thinking that we should be the world's police force.

I love this country, and I love the American people. However, the American people are distinct from the U.S. government and its policies.

The hate directed toward the U.S. is not meant for the people of America, but for the U.S. government and its policies. We, the American people, do have the power to change our government, but it will be a difficult and uphill struggle that will require many sacrifices. We cannot afford to put it off any longer. We have to unite America or let the power-hungry Global Elite lead us to our death and the end of this great Republic.

PART IV

The few who can understand the system will be so interested in its profits, or so dependent on its favors, that there will be no opposition from that class, while on the other hand, the great body of the people are mentally incapable of comprehending the tremendous advantage that derives from the system, will bear its burdens without complaint, and perhaps without even suspecting that the system is inimical to their interests.

—Rothschild Brothers of London in a series of letters between Senator John Sherman and the brothers Rothschild, to start a new Central Bank in America, June 1863

So long as the people do not care to exercise their freedom, those who wish to tyrannize will do so; for tyrants are active and ardent, and will devote themselves in the name of any number of gods, religious and otherwise, to put shackles upon sleeping men.

—Voltairine de Cleyre

21

PEOPLE OF THE LIE

There can be little doubt that our politicians are addicted to power. However, it is the Global Elite who are pulling the strings and setting the agenda for a New World Order. They are the true power brokers of this world, and they have been working their plan for generations, employing the propaganda techniques pioneered by Willi Munzenberg under Lenin and Stalin. They are determined to divide and conquer America in order to succeed. Never has it been more apparent than during the 2004 election as they kept the conservatives and the liberals at each other's throats. They manipulated the political landscape to make it feel as if the Red states and the Blue states were fighting a civil war.

Their tactic is to energize as many issues as possible to foster disagreement between the two sides, and their fingerprints were all over the sixties free speech movement. Many would say that this Global Elite is a Communist organization that worked its magic to sway people like John Kerry and Jane Fonda to its cause during the Vietnam War. But that is not true. This powerful group has one long range goal—global domination—and they will use whichever tool will work best to achieve their aims. Hate, anger, and controversy are their tools in trade.

The people who got us into the Vietnam War and benefited enormously from it are the heads of the military/industrial complex, members of the Global Elite. They also instigated protest marches and the burning of draft cards to create a controversy with the Nixon administration and hasten the growth of the police state. They know how to create controversy and how to profit from it. They played one side against the other for an even bigger payoff down the road. This shadow group knows that to strip the American people of their Constitutional protections they have to do it slowly, over time, like Chinese water torture, until the tide is solidly in their favor. This is a group of such power and secrecy that 50 years earlier Woodrow Wilson had cautioned that this group should only be criticized in a whisper.

The United States did not enter the war in Vietnam to win. It was a war to weaken the United States in its struggle against the Soviet Union as the Elite played one side against the other. In the years since Vietnam I have heard many officers who served there complain that they never understood what our policies were or why we never fought the war as though we wanted to win. Instead we fought a defensive struggle to save South Vietnam, playing by their rules, engaging in a guerrilla war on their turf. The idea of fighting a limited war on their terms, as opposed to a war based on our strengths, was insane!

Had we wanted to win the war we would have gone into Hanoi with a thousand tanks and wiped it off the map, or we would have napalmed it until it was toast. Hanoi was where the money came from—the heart of the beast—and had we destroyed the heart, the tentacles would have shriveled up and died. If the intent had been to win, we would have used our strength to destroy Hanoi. You either fight to win or you don't fight unless you absolutely have to; any military officer will tell you that. Once again the secret power merchants in Washington were involved, sacrificing nations and their people like pawns in a chess game in pursuit of their political and financial interests.

The Global Elite will take the hot political issues of the day, and then mix parenting, God, gay rights, civil rights, and/or religion into the pot as part of a media campaign to start a war of ideas and controversy. The result is the current Red State / Blue State divide. Like Willi Munzenberg, they are always on the prowl for recruits, playing into their issues of guilt or greed as they simultaneously seduce and brainwash them. The progressive elites of the New Deal era were easy targets for them, as many of them lived aristocratic lifestyles while harboring guilt about family money that came from slave trading and opium.

I believe that Bill and Hillary are willing participants in this strategy to subvert America and all that it stands for. In his book *The Seduction of Hillary Rodham*, David Brock describes many of the people who helped them along in their political careers. One of Hillary's first missions was to promote the rights of children over their parents' authority. A brilliant woman, she was able to use the court's inability to properly deal with this issue as a means to leverage her authority against parental rights. From here it was an easy step to demand that children be given the right to make their own decisions regarding health care, schooling, and employment, over parental opposition. Hillary was able to use the liberal court system as a means to drive a wedge into the traditional family makeup.

Here is an example of what is happening in America: A California law currently forbids a child under 14 to get a tattoo or smoke without parental consent. But if a 13-year-old girl gets pregnant, she is allowed to leave school to get an abortion—and her teachers are forbidden by law from informing her parents.

Which has the potential to be more harmful to a 13-year-old girl, an abortion or a tattoo? Just like Willi under Stalin, the goal is to select your opponent, vilify their position, and then champion the cause of the other side by claiming that they are on the side of freedom (in this case, protecting the rights of a young 13-year-old girl from her parents). This is part of a very serious effort to break up the family, to destroy the most basic bond holding our society together. The destruction of the family makes it easier for the state to play the role of God.

The push for globalization has recently gained tremendous momentum, and there have been relatively few challenges from anyone in our government. The concept of globalization has been sold to America, in subtle and not-so-subtle ways, as the ideal and inevitable direction of our future—without ever questioning the ends or the means by which we get there. As a Republic, we are based on representation, and we have been totally unrepresented in this momentous process.

The Global Elite is the most evil and intelligent group of people that have ever lived, and their End Game is now in sight. They have been behind the scenes pulling the strings behind every major war in the last century. What they did in Vietnam is very similar to the way they pulled the strings in the Middle East, playing Iraq against Iran for 10 years, depleting both countries emotionally, economically, and politically. For 10 years the CIA trained Osama bin Laden. And now we are fighting him.

It is interesting to note that in 1996 President Clinton assigned the U.S. intelligence community a new role, that of fighting global crime. He divided our intelligence community into two groups; one had the traditional role of gathering foreign intelligence while the second group began a new role of fighting global crime. This second group would support the United Nations police keeping efforts. On May 13 1996 the Washington Inquirer reported that the National Security Council created two new committees: The Foreign Intelligence Committee and the Global Crime Committee.

The Irony here is that Clinton had several opportunities to capture bin Laden and passed them up. In a 2001 article in the Los Angeles Times article dated December 5, Mansoor Ijaz explained in detail how, between 1996 and 1998, he met with officials in the Clinton administration, including Sandy Berger, the National Security advisor, and offered bin Laden to be arrested on behalf of the Sudanese government. Again in July of 2000, after the Embassy bombings and just before the Cole bombing, Ijaz tried to offer bin Laden up to the Clinton administration, but once again they ignored the opportunity.

Clinton has become something of a folk hero to the Left, but what they may not understand is that Clinton did more to further the plans of the Global Elite than any President in recent history. He did this deliberately and intentionally, and for that they continue to praise him, and yet the members of the liberal Left fail to appreciate how they are being manipulated.

The Global Elite has taken the liberal Left from the sixties and given it a radical makeover. They have transformed it from a group that was all about freedom of speech and the rights of the individual into a group that is now using political correctness to obstruct the values they once stood for. In her book *The Death Of Right And Wrong*, Tammy Bruce describes how the cultural elite has demonized our understanding of decency in order to lobotomize Americans into a foggy silence. I believe that Bruce is misidentifying the source of the disinformation. It is the Global Elite that is the power behind the radical Left, as they utilize political correctness as a means of obscuring the line between right and wrong.

This shadow group is capitalizing on the weak and the wounded of our society. The victims of this group are individuals who have suffered abuse and trauma early in life, whether in infancy, childhood, or adolescence. The pathology they suffer is narcissism, an excessive infatuation and obsession with oneself to the exclusion of others.

Bruce describes the plight of a deaf lesbian couple who themselves are mental health therapists. They were so self-involved that they thought it would be wonderful to produce a deaf child to satisfy their own narcissistic needs. They used the sperm of a man who is also deaf to increase their chances of conceiving a deaf child, never giving any thought to the fact that they were deliberately inflicting a disability onto this child for their own selfish purposes. They might claim they were trying to perpetuate their deaf culture, but they had really decided to play God! This is the extent to which the thought police have succeeded in obscuring the line between right and wrong. So far, this child has failed his hearing tests and is deaf.

This pathology of the Global Elite is especially disgusting because people who have been victimized early in life are not encouraged to seek the professional help they desperately need, but instead are further abused to achieve the political goals of their leaders. In effect, those who need professional help the most are taught to celebrate their wounds as if they were badges of courage. Yet the leaders are now the ones inflicting trauma, and the healing process becomes more difficult. Bruce applies the term *malignant narcissism* to these leaders who further exploit the love, trust and confidence of these already wounded souls. Recovery becomes the enemy as a wounded psyche furthers a radical political agenda.

Needless to say, in a position of power these people can pose a threat to society, political stability, and world order. From personal experience, Bruce describes how she has witnessed leaders in the feminist, gay rights, and civil rights movements exercise this malignant narcissism to further their political agendas by exploiting their own people and issues. These insights don't come from an outsider throwing stones at her detractors, but from a woman who, as the head of the N.O.W. organization in L.A. for almost seven years, was very much an insider.

All of this is done to obscure our understanding of right and wrong. The claim is that because we may not share a similar cultural background or sexual orientation, we cannot stand in judgment of behavior that is immoral or even criminal, as though our values were invalid and our morals no longer applied. Bruce points out that it is the degradation of our basic moral template that allows people like Bill Clinton and Jesse Jackson to be held up by the Media Elite as examples of their modern-day foot soldiers.

The radical Left seems intent on destroying the very fabric of the traditional family, the central core of any society or civilization. If you destroy this, you wreak havoc on the foundation, and everything else comes tumbling down soon after. Willi Munzenberg lives on in the Global Elite.

In his book *Tragedy and Hope: History of the World in Our Time* Carroll Quigley details J.P. Morgan's infiltration of the Left-wing political movements in the early 20th century. These groups were starved for money, and Morgan provided them with funds as he tracked their development. Quigley states that any power they exercised was not their own but was ultimately the power of an elite group of international bankers. Quigley states that this power structure penetrated deeply into university life, the press, and the foreign policy of the United States.

It was Quigley who convinced Clinton to apply for a Rhodes scholarship at Oxford. Quigley was an associate of Madeline Albright on the Georgetown University faculty, and Clinton's favorite professor. Quigley claims that he studied the international bankers, including Morgan, for 20 years, and that they allowed him to examine their secret records and papers for two years during the sixties. Except for a few of their tactics, Quigley claims that he is in agreement with their objectives for a one-world government.

Consider the following situation, described by Gary Aldrich in *Unlimited Access*. Bill Clinton was late for his own inauguration because he was fighting with Hillary over the site of her office. When Hillary discovered Bill's affair with Gennifer Flowers, she demanded her pound of flesh, which was to occupy the office normally held by the Vice President. When Al Gore refused to give up his office, the Clintons got into an argument just prior to the inauguration ceremonies. One policeman described Hillary as screaming at Bill with "uncontrolled and unbridled fury." According to Aldrich, it was agreed that to mollify

Hillary she would be given authority over staff hiring and domestic policy. That sounds like malignant narcissism to me.

Here is another example from Gary Aldrich. He was asked to help decorate the Christmas tree for the Blue Room at the White House in 1993. They were to use Hillary's box of ornaments, which included two male figurines with erections, turtle doves fornicating, crack pipes and other drug paraphernalia, gold-wrapped condoms, and sex toys known as cock rings. The intent was to denigrate, to tarnish the office of the Presidency, the symbol of America to the world.

In his book *SCAM, How the Black Leadership Exploits Black America*, Reverend Jesse Lee Peterson details how the African American community has been demeaned in the name of good, pointing out that Jesse Jackson and Al Sharpton have made a living by exploiting other African Americans. This black leadership has very little interest in solving the problems of other African Americans because they make a profit off them. Jesse Jackson once threatened to condemn a large merger in the Telecom industry because it hurt black workers. However, after he received a million-dollar contribution to his coalition he was more than happy to give it his blessing.

Bill Cosby has long been an advocate for the African American community, encouraging them to address the very real problems that face their community. Mr. Cosby has had the courage and compassion to speak up, even in the face of harsh criticism, to try and deal with some very critical issues, while many of his critics find it more profitable to ignore the problems. Reverend Peterson has described this as *black racism*, something that Booker T. Washington spoke of almost a century ago.

I believe all Americans deserve to be treated with the utmost respect, dignity, and fairness, no matter their race, skin color, religion, or sexual preference. But that does not give anyone the right to use their differences as a club to deprive other individuals of their rights or liberties. By the same token I do not believe that the Christian Right has the moral authority to condemn a person for getting an abortion. They are entitled to their beliefs, but they do not have any right or authority to claim that it is murder. There are many religions that believe Soul enters the body during the last stages of pregnancy, and has very little contact with the fetus in the first several months of conception. This is a religious belief held by hundreds of millions of people who believe in karma and reincarnation.

The Global Elite represents the darkest chapter in the history of world politics. They are slowly seducing the Declaration of Independence and our Constitution right out from under us. When the dust has cleared and we are a small part of a huge global empire, what will we have to protect us from the tyranny of these monsters? As Americans, we represent the last possible opportunity to stop them, to halt this madness. If America falls prey to their seductive message, it could mean the end of the free world as we know it. Only by coming together as Americans, by celebrating and protecting the liberty we cherish, can we pass this dream on to our children.

22

THE SOUND OF ONE HAND CLAPPING

In his book *The Bubble of American Supremacy*, George Soros offers an excellent and well-researched account of the neoconservatives and their plan for global American supremacy. This plan has been embraced by Bush and is responsible for the current war in Iraq.

One of Soros' concerns is that the war in Iraq will prevent future efforts at nation building, which he favors. Had Kerry been elected, it is likely that Soros would have had some role in the administration, helping to determine where large portions of American taxpayer dollars would have gone to further democracy by means of nation building. It appears that his main criticism of Bush is that Bush used a unilateral military approach to nation building, as opposed to the Soros approach that favors the carrot instead of the stick.

Soros is a nation builder with a humanitarian outlook and an obviously Left-leaning bias, though like many people he believes that pulling out of Iraq will severely damage our image, as happened in Vietnam. But this will be worse, he says, because of our dependence on oil from the Middle East. Soros agreed with the invasion of Afghanistan, yet disagreed with Rumsfeld's refusal to allow the U.N. peacekeepers to get involved. He describes this as a failed opportunity for the world to see a brilliant demonstration of what international assistance can do for a Muslim country. Not to argue with such an intelligent man, but when has the U.N. ever done anything that could be described as brilliant?

Early in his book, on page 10, Soros explains, *"It is only natural for politicians to twist, exploit, or manipulate events to promote their policies"* (italics mine). I wonder, does Soros now consider himself a politician, or just a lobbyist? And do lobbyists use the same tactics as politicians? I believe there is very little difference between the two.

Soros' main effort at nation building is through his Open Society Institute (OSI) that aims to promote open societies by reshaping government policy and supporting education, media, public health, and human and women's rights, as well as social, legal, and economic reform. In order to comply with U.S. law, Soros states on his OSI web site, www.soros.org, that his private political activities are wholly separate from OSI, which is a nonpartisan, nonpolitical entity. But I would hypothesize that he is actually working toward the same goal in both instances: promoting globalization and a one-world government.

When he was running for President, the senior Bush spoke of a New World Order that was beginning to take shape, as evidenced by his own actions to fight a war against Saddam Hussein. He accepted U.N. authorization instead of seeking Congressional approval. But there was such a negative reaction to his use of the phrase *New World Order* that he stopped using those words and instead began to talk about the *globalization* of the world. He meant the same thing; he just had to use a different term to make it more palatable.

In part II of his book Soros presents his personal vision, which acknowledges that the international financiers and the multinationals have a big advantage in the global marketplace because they are so nimble and flexible. On page 91 he says, "It is dangerous, however, to place excessive reliance on the market mechanism. Markets are designed to facilitate the free exchange of goods and services among willing participants, but are not capable, on their own, of taking care of *collective needs* (italics mine)." His primary purpose is to provide a more humanitarian rationale for international intervention into the affairs of the various countries around the world that need his help. He wants to play God on a grand scale.

In effect, Soros begins making the case for a global welfare state, and like FDR, he believes that intelligent people such as he are best suited to socially engineer the economic, cultural, and spiritual needs of the world. He starts by stating that the U.S. needs to bend over backward to regain the trust and allegiance of the rest of the world. My position of adopting neutrality would, in the long run, be less expensive and go further to heal the wounds caused by our foreign policy.

Soros goes on to propose that a community of democracies within the U.N. form a democratic bloc that would exclude countries like Syria or Libya from chairing important commissions. He puts it like this on page 120: "Repressive regimes would be excluded from active decision making; failed states could be put under the protection of the United Nations." He then proposes that a community of emerging democracies form a separate coalition, independent of the U.S., to replace the G77 group. These two groups would work together as equals to multilaterally end world conflict and promote international peace. Of course the large countries would have to pay higher dues.

Soros then proceeds on a philosophical discussion of his Open Society and capitalism. He refers to the provisions of the Declaration of Independence as being part of his Open Society, but distinguishes between the idealism of the Open Society and the lack thereof in free market capitalism. He criticized President Bush when, in March of 2002, he pledged five billion dollars to the Millennium Challenge Account for developing countries, because it was unilateral and would go to the wrong kind of countries.

My criticism is that the U.S. is eight trillion dollars in debt, and that debt continues to mount each day. The U.N. is a breeding ground for corruption, and we already flush more than seven billion dollars down the U.N. toilet every year. What does it accomplish? Just continued demands for more money with nothing to show for it. Then Bush decided that the U.N. could do a better job than the U.S. distributing the $350 million we gave to the Tsunami relief effort. Had he forgotten the Oil for Food scandal already? Fortunately, Price Waterhouse stepped in.

Toward the end of his book Soros states that the U.S. has a huge advantage in the race for military superiority, but that the rest of the world is trying to catch up. He offers his solution on page 175: "We (the U.S.) are in a position to dictate the terms that would satisfy us. We are prevented from doing so only by our own attitude: nothing would satisfy us because, under the influence of extremists, we are opposed to the process." *By extremists, he is referring to those of us who wish to preserve and protect the liberty guaranteed by the Constitution of the United States.*

He claims that the arms race could be slowed down by a rigorously monitored international agreement. The U.N. has never done anything rigorously except support fraud, corruption, lies, and deceit. How stupid does Soros think Americans are? Soros calls himself an American who truly loves his country, but at the same time he is just a little furious that we won't disregard a little thing like our Constitutional heritage! So we have to ask, what is the real Soros agenda?

Soros attended the London School of Economics, an early target of the secret societies previously referred to as the Group. Members of secret societies that go back hundreds of years formed all of the previously discussed secret orders: the CFR, the Bilderbergs, and the Trilateral Commission. Both George Soros and Bill Clinton belong to all three of the above organizations, which I refer to as the Elite Three. Most Americans would only recognize a couple of the names that belong to all three groups, such as Paul Volker or Henry Kissenger.

There is the Lenin School of Marxism and then there is the Fabian school, which resides at the London School of Economics. Their model was based on the tactics of Roman General Quintus Fabius Maximus Verrucosus, who kept Hannibal at bay in the second century B.C. by avoiding confrontation whenever possible. He wore down the opposing army by maneuvering to stall the conflict. Their symbol was the turtle and on their shield was a wolf in sheep's clothing. The Fabian Marxists are willing to work quietly and patiently from within the organization that is their target. Their approach to spreading socialism is not quite so brutal as that of Lenin and Stalin. Like the Roman general of old, the Fabians employ the symbology of the turtle and the wolf in sheep's clothing.

Fabian members included George Bernard Shaw, Arnold Toynebee, and H.G. Wells, who even wrote about it in his book *The Open Conspiracy*. Wells spelled out in minute detail how it was possible to embed collectivism into society without arousing alarm or suspicion. The Fabian group was involved in the Bolshevik Revolution but had been appalled at the amount of killing and violence. They have the same goal as Lenin's group but employ subtler tactics. They want the old religions to make way for the new religion, which is the state, and the masses will continue to be led by the ruling Elite.

Another interesting twist is that Karl Marx, long thought to be the author of the *Communist Manifesto*, in fact plagiarized the work from an obscure French socialist, according to Anthony C. Sutton in his book *The Federal Reserve Conspiracy*. The Frenchman was named Victor Considerant and his work was *Principes du Socialisme: Manifeste de la Democratie au DixNeuvieme Seicle*. The first edition was published in 1843 and the second edition in 1847 in Paris, where Marx and Engels were living at the time. The plagiarism was first spotted by another obscure writer, W. Tcherkesoff, in his book *Pages of Socialist History*.

The Manifesto is a blueprint for class warfare between the proletariat and the bourgeoisie, whereby the political and economic power reside with an elite few. Marxism really has nothing to do with relieving the misery of the poor and advancing mankind, but instead is a way for the cunning and wealthy to consolidate their grip on power. It turns out that Marx was financed by a group of wealthy American bankers and members of the German aristocracy, who used a pirate from Louisiana called Jean Laffite to act as the go-between. Although the Encyclopedia Britannica claims that Laffite died in 1823, Sutton claims that they are wrong and that Laffite went underground in 1820 when he became a courier for American bankers.

Why would bankers want to see Communism take over the world? They don't. This is just another clever ploy to further their plan. Point number 5 of the measures laid out by Marx is: *Centralization of credit in the hands of the State, by means of a national bank with State capital and an exclusive monopoly.* The devil might say this was pure genius; International bankers playing one side against the other, financing both sides and using both sides to further your ultimate goal, complete control and domination of the game!

There is an even more powerful and elite group of individuals that keeps no written names of its members. These would be the ultimate Puppet Masters.

Fox News released Paul Volker's first findings in relation to the Oil For Food scandal on Sunday evening, January 9, 2005. Volker was quoted as saying he hadn't found any smoking gun. The report stated that the U.N. was billed for 1800 days of salary during the time that the Oil for Food fraud was taking place, by employees who did not show up for work. This cost the U.N. $1.4 million dollars in false salary payments. But this figure is dwarfed by the $21 billion that Saddam scammed while these employees were not on the job. And Volker (CFR,BB,TC) says there was no smoking gun?!

The OSI is all about Soros using personal finances to spread democracy in the rest of the world as he helps to prepare for the New World Order, a one-world government that would be run with a single economic plan and legal system administered by the United Nations. He has a 10-year plan to speed up the development of Eastern and Central Europe, as well as Mongolia and the Middle East, to get them ready for the Open Society he is promoting. His activities could well be termed priming the pump for the New World Order. In this way Soros is using his wealth to influence the course of American politics.

Another Soros subgroup is the Center on Crime, created by the OSI. For this Soros put up $300,000 to finance a successful Brooklyn lawsuit against gun manufacturers. The point here is to find the manufacturer guilty of a crime, as opposed to the person who fired the gun. The continued efforts to eliminate the concept of personal responsibility in our society are part of the reason for its breakdown. The reason the Global Elite think it important to take guns out of the hands of Americans is to make it easier for the New World Order to establish its authority. Remember, one of the first things the Nazis did was to take the guns away from the citizens.

Soros will use any available means, including the women's movement, to further his cause. By getting American women to sympathize with and become involved in women's rights issues around the world, Soros is attempting to distract them from the liberties being stolen from them right here at home. This is another Willi Munzenberg tactic to divide American society and make it easier to get support for globalization.

Although the membership lists are public, the organizations of the Global Elite are very private, and it is impossible to know who is behind the scenes making the important decisions and pulling the strings. Ross' book *Who's Who of the Elite* is an excellent resource to use while watching the news and other "unbiased" media stories to see how many members of the Global Elite you can spot. What illusions are they trying to sell you? The Ross book also lists the corporate sponsors of the Global Elite, and that list is substantial.

The Global Elite has been telling us whom to elect for President for decades. In 1992 both Bush senior and Clinton were really representing the CFR. Surprisingly, Al Gore does not have what it takes to become a member.

So when we hear Soros criticizing President Bush, doesn't it sound a lot like one hand clapping? I would again hypothesize that President Bush is ultimately after the same goal as Soros, he is just using a different strategy. Are Bush and Soros really two sides of the same coin? Could it be that the Bush plan to spread democracy by means of the warfare state is simply his way of accomplishing the same goal as Soros, who is employing the welfare state strategy? Both men are part of a secret society that wants to gain control of the world. This isn't just about the Left versus the Right in America. It is about the Global Elite playing Monopoly and employing Willi Munzenberg propaganda strategies to win a rigged game.

Granted, it is possible that Mr. Soros is the world's most altruistic billionaire, giving from the bottom of his heart, and my hypothesis is wrong. If that is the case, then he is simply an unwitting participant in the dark shadows of the Global elite, a pawn being used like so many others.

But let me quote another member of the Elite Three, Henry Kissinger, from a speech he made at a Bilderberg meeting in Evian, France, in 1992: "Today Americans would be outraged if U.N. troops entered Los Angeles to restore order; tomorrow they will be grateful! This is especially true if they were told that there was an outside threat from beyond, whether real or promulgated, that threatened our very existence. It is then that all people of the world will plead with world leaders to deliver them from this evil. The one thing every man fears is the unknown. When presented with this scenario, individual rights will be willingly relinquished for the guarantee of their well being granted to them by their world government." Kissinger rubs elbows with Soros and Paul Wolfowitz at the meetings of the CFR, BB, and TC. You be the judge.

The Global Elite currently have three members of our Supreme Court in their pocket. Stephen Breyer, Ruth Bader Ginsberg, and Sandra Day O'Connor all belong to the CFR. Thus it is no wonder that the Judiciary has become the de facto legislative branch of the land. It will be extremely interesting to see whom Bush decides to put on the Supreme Court when he has the chance.

Like the brilliant magician/psychotherapists they are, the Elite don't care whether the Left or the Right wins. Both sides are intent on stealing our liberty once and for all: the Left by taking away economic liberty via taxation and social welfare systems, and the Right by means of war and such measures as the Patriot Act. But this much is certain: their plan, if successful, will mean the end of the American Dream.

23

THE ORDER OF SKULL AND BONES

There is a society, a secret society, on the Yale Campus, that selects 15 new male members each year. Men cannot apply for membership but can only be selected. Each candidate is observed during his first three years as an undergraduate, and then chosen to enter for his senior year. In his book *America's Secret Establishment*, Anthony C. Sutton gives us an insightful look into this extremely secret society and some of what little has ever been disclosed about it.

The candidate is energetic, resourceful, political, and most likely an amoral team player who will sacrifice himself for the good of the team. Loners and individualists are not what the group is looking for. At any given time only about one quarter of the members are active, and over the 170 years since its inception, some 20 to 30 families have emerged to dominate the Order of Skull and Bones.

The families fall into two groups. The old-line families who arrived here in the 1600s, such as Whitney, Lord, Bundy, and Adams form the first group. The second group includes families that acquired their wealth in the last 150 years, sent their sons to Yale, and have become almost old-line families themselves. They include the likes of Rockefeller, Harriman, and Payne. There is a lot of intermarriage between these families.

A familiar pattern is that of Brown Brothers, Harriman, a small international banking firm started in 1800 in New York and Philadelphia. According to Sutton, by the 1970s they had taken in so many of the Brotherhood that no fewer than nine of the individual partners were members of the Order. We see similar patterns at other companies, such as Standard Oil, Weyerhaeuser, Pillsbury, and J.P. Morgan. The one thing all members swear to in secrecy is that their loyalty to the Order is above all other loyalties, including the university.

The cofounders of the Skull and Bones were Alfonso Taft, whose son would become President in 1913 and then later a Supreme Court Justice, and William Huntington Russell. These men set up a trust to fund the Order, and this fund is managed by Brown Brothers, Harriman. Each member of the Order is given $15,000 and powerful connections with which to get started in life and make their mark.

William H. Russell is the cousin of Samuel Russell, who founded Russell and Company, a shipping business that made immense fortunes in the China trade by buying opium from Turkey and then shipping it to China. Russell's chief of operations was Warren Delano Jr., grandfather of FDR. Joseph Coolidge was another Russell investor. It was his son that started United Fruit, which maintained the colonial interests of many of New England's most influential families. It was Coolidge's grandson, Archibald C. Coolidge, who founded the Council on Foreign Relations, CFR.

Senator Prescott Bush and his son George H.W. Bush were both Bonesmen. Prescott, who served in Army intelligence, was close to the Rockefellers and the Harrimans. In his book *Secret Societies of America's Elite*, Sora relates that when George W. Bush was tapped to become a member of Skull and Bones, he told a friend that he would rather be a member of the Gin and Tonic Order. His father, George H.W., anticipating such a response, knocked on his son's door at 8 P.M. that night and told him it was time to do the right thing and become a "good man." George W. Bush, class of 1968, did become a Bonesman.

Senator John Forbes Kerry was a Bonesman, class of 1966, whose ancestors were among the opium pioneers in China, according to Sora. John Heinz II, a Bonesman class of 1931, was father to Senator John Heinz III, who was killed in a mysterious plane crash on the same day Senator Tower was killed in a separate plane crash. They had both allegedly been involved in negotiations with Iran over the captured hostages in 1979. Senator Heinz III's wife, Teresa, was a member of the Council on Foreign Relations when she inherited $860 million. She later married another Bonesman, Senator Kerry.

Sutton looks at the influence of the Order on all aspects of American society. He details how the Order took control of Yale University and how they have corrupted the American educational system. He examines the great lengths the Order has gone to in order to gain control of the content in American schools. Sutton shows how the Order has placed an emphasis on global living and diversity, instead of giving American children the best possible education.

It is no secret that almost every university campus in America is a bastion of liberal beliefs and ideologies, heavily influenced by the Order's agenda. This philosophy holds that education should not be child-centered, but state-centered, to best meet the needs of the state. This brainwashing process has been gaining steam since public education became mandatory after World War II, with the specific goal of implementing their New World Order.

The cornerstone of the Order's influence comes from John Dewey, the arch-creator of modern educational theory. Dewey's philosophy was very much influenced by Hegel, the German philosopher who believed that the individual could best be used to serve the state. Sutton points out that if Dewey had tried to achieve today's educational system through legislation, it would have been found unconstitutional. Instead it was achieved by the injection of massive private funds from foundations under the influence, and sometimes the control of the Order. These include the Ford, Carnegie, Rockefeller, Peabody, Sloan, Slater, and Twentieth Century Foundations, among others.

The Order has had a knack for rising to the head of large private funds. It has long been its policy to start as many influential organizations as possible and then to control their direction. Members of the Order or persons close to the Order have started the American Historical Association, The American Economic Association, The American Chemical Association, and The American Psychological Association. In 1920 William Howard Taft, a member of the Order, became the first Chairman of the American Society for the Judicial Settlement of International Disputes. These organizations have become vital in their efforts to condition society over the years, to tell America what it should believe and value. The Establishment often ridicules ideas that don't conform to their concepts right out of existence.

Using tax-exempt foundations to achieve what appear to be noble goals is another way of deceiving the public into an almost hypnotic state where it appears that everything is perfectly fine and the "good guys" are working to improve the system. When the decision was reached to control the domestic educational system, another tax-exempt fund was recruited. The Carnegie Foundation approached the Guggenheim Foundation with an offer to sponsor 20 of their Ph.D. candidates in American history. They went looking for candidates who were sympathetic to the idea of a collective society based on socialistic principles. The students were instructed that if they accepted the grants they would then be required to spend their teaching careers supporting and defending their positions within the structure of American history. Thus was a cunningly successful program to put another layer of the onion into place, further corrupting the educational system. It would appear that the only way to stop this deception is to remove tax-exempt status from all foundations.

The Order has worked to set its agenda in every American institution, from the media to medicine and politics. The major New York law firms are filled with members of the Order. Henry Luce of Time-Life was a member, as is William Buckley of *The National Review*, as was Richard Ely Danielson of *Atlantic Monthly*, as was Russell Wheeler of *Fortune*. Pierre Jay, the first chairman of the New York Federal Reserve, was a member. So far three Presidents have come from the Order: William Taft and both Bushes. The odds against this happening by chance are incredible.

It is my belief that the Order had been in existence for centuries under various guises. It probably decided to follow the lead of the Group, from Oxford, as America's universities began to flourish. These secret societies in Europe and America have connections that go back at least several centuries, if not further.

According to Sutton, the key to modern history is this: the Global Elitists had close working relationships with both the Marxists and the Nazis, and were instrumental in supporting the rise of these philosophies in Germany and Russia. And they were also responsible for their destruction.

Both Nazism and Communism are based on the principles of Hegel. In order to create a New World Order employing Hegelian philosophy, one needs dialectic, a conflict that can be used to further the stated or non-stated objectives. Sutton details how the Left and the Right have been used to fund and finance war and revolution on the domestic front and abroad to foster their aim of a global government.

The dialectic process consists of conflict between opposing forces. Any idea may be seen as *thesis*, which will encourage an opposing force, known as *antithesis*. The final outcome will be a *synthesis* of the two conflicting forces. J. P. Morgan attended college for two or three years in the mid-1850s at the University of Gottingen, Germany. This was a center of Hegelian activism, which J.P. Morgan used in all of his dealings with the various political parties. He was always able to keep a foot in both camps.

Although Morgan was not a member of the Order, at his death his company became Morgan, Stanley & Co. The Stanley was Harold Stanley, a member of the Order, class of 1908. Sutton traces the influence of the Order on the Left through Guaranty Trust Company, which Morgan had his fingers in, and Brown Brothers Harriman, which used a joint venture called Ruskobank to support the Bolshevik Revolution and the evolutionary development of the Soviet Union. On the Right, Guaranty Trust & Co. and Union Banking Group (Harriman and Nazi interests) were involved in Hitler's ascension to power and the subsidy of National Socialism. Sutton supplies extensive detail in regard to well-known members of the Order and their financial institutions. Western textbooks have been carefully censored to eliminate any mention of Western assistance to Hitler. Much of the evidence for Western support for Stalin has also been deleted from our textbooks, but can be found in Anthony Sutton's book *The Best Enemy That Money Can Buy*.

Averill Harriman was the elder statesman of the Democratic Party, and a member of the Order, class of 1913, while George H.W. Bush was the champion of the Republican Party, a member of the Order, and class of 1949. The principal devices used to control the dialectic process have been information, war, debt, and technology. This has kept the two parties locked in a phony struggle between Left and Right, which keeps the real issue out of the public spotlight. The most important struggle is the battle for individual freedom against the encroaching power of the absolute state, which the Global Elite wants to hide.

Never has this been so transparent as in the 2004 election, between two members of the Order of the Skull and Bones, when verbal animosity and bitterness reached historic proportions. The end result of this conflict between the Left and the Right is to promote a subliminal image of the state as God. As long as the Global Elite are in control of the government, they can play God at their leisure, no matter which side wins.

It is hard to imagine a more diabolical plan to gain global power. Sutton explains that *Skull & Bones is not American at all; it is a branch of a foreign secret society that has but one allegiance: itself.* The followers of the Left and the Right are unconscious pawns being used by the Global Elite in a dialectical conflict to further its goal: divide and conquer. The ideas and strategies of Willi Munzenberg have met with incredible success in fanning the flames of controversy and driving the Red States further from the Blue States. The more hate, anger, and bitterness become a part of the conflict, the quicker their victory and a New World Order.

On one level it sounds utterly fantastic that the Puppet Masters could be so determined to increase their already enormous wealth that they care nothing for the millions of people who have died in countless unnecessary wars over the last few centuries. But some people's desire to rule the world is obviously very old, and evidently quite strong.

24

IF YOU WANT TO DESTROY A COUNTRY, DESTROY ITS MEMORY

Milan Kundera

Milan Kundera, a Czechoslovakian who watched Stalin murder his Catholic friends, has seen what the politics of fear and hate can do. But the politics of fear and hate proliferated by someone like Stalin are more easily detected than when a country is slowly plundered from the inside by lies and disinformation. Even more treacherous than that is the situation that arises when the lies are proffered as universal truths that linger always around the next corner, the next war.

As Americans, I believe most of us treasure our First Amendment rights of free speech. But what if I told you that one of your inalienable rights was to be free from want? Do you think that would be reasonable? And what if I promised that another of your inalienable rights was to be free from fear? Would you say I was crazy, that no one could guarantee this? You would be absolutely right.

And finally, what if I told you that it was America's obligation to provide the rest of the world with the same inalienable rights that U.S. citizens enjoy, and that we also had to guarantee them freedom from want and fear? You would have me committed on the spot. And yet this is exactly the burden FDR placed on our shoulders when he obligated all Americans to fulfill the Four Freedoms, upon which he based the United Nations. Ever the political genius, he put this forward as his *New Deal for the world*. FDR saw no end to his power and glory; big government and a Machiavellian determination were his tools.

In the Winter, 2004 Issue of *The Hoover Digest*, Charles Hill describes President Bush's policy of preemption and his efforts this past year as a "resurrection of the U.N." He declares that this reawakening will help the U.S. government to convince the Europeans of the deadly threat posed to their way of life by a Middle East in the grip of political and religious pathologies.

For all those on the Right who see the U.S. government as the military savior of the world, I am sure this makes logical sense. There are those who believe that Bush can create a democratic way of life in the Mideast and other parts of the world where none has existed before. But how long are we going to let our soldiers come home in body bags to support the neoconservative ideology of U.S. imperialism?

Paul Wolfowitz is the Deputy Defense Secretary for President Bush and one of the architects of the neoconservative philosophy that is pushing for the American military supremacy that Mr. Soros refers to. He is also in the Elite Three as a member of the CFR, BB, and TC. *The Hoover Digest* at Stanford University is filled with members who belong to one or more of these secret groups.

Having the backing of the United Nations would indeed lend a bit of legitimacy to Bush's supreme effort to democratize the world and thus defeat terrorism. George Hill would have us believe that the free world has to mobilize to avoid World War III. But this is a certain formula for disaster. The U.N. has not yet even been able to define the word "terrorism."

With Bush claiming the moral authority of a righteous and religious war, what we really have is the Crusades all over again. Both the Muslim extremists and the West will be claiming to have God on their side. I would suggest that World War III may have already started, and the neoconservatives on the Right are already dropping hints that they are about to begin bombing Iran.

On the Left are the thought police who are using their cause of cultural diversity and socialistic propaganda in an attempt to destroy the foundations of our Republic as they slouch towards Gomorrah and globalization. If you buy into this groupthink, then you believe the world's population will experience a higher standard of living and the planet will be at peace.

Both parties allow for the multinational corporations to reign supreme as they divide up the world and its natural resources. The only difference will be that once the New World Government (NWG) is imposed, their campaign contributions will be given to the officers of the United Nations instead of to Congressmen. Congress has already abdicated its authority to the President and the Judicial branch of the government, so abdicating to the U.N will be easy for them. Marrying the American bureaucracy to the U.N. bureaucracy will create a catastrophic nightmare.

The U.N. represents hypocrisy of such an incredible magnitude that it is contaminating the heart and soul of America. The longer we continue to perpetuate this cancer, the more our national memory and heritage will be lost, and our ideals sacrificed upon the altar of constant warfare.

At the U.N. Millennium Summit in New York September 6-8, 2000, 150 world leaders met to begin the process of transforming the U.N. into the New World Government. These leaders signed 40 different treaties, conventions, and protocols on international law that began the process of establishing this NWG. In his book *The New World Order Exposed*, Robert Montgomery quotes former KGB officer Anatoly Golitsyn, who said in 1991 that "Soviet strategists will come forward with fresh initiatives combined with deliberate provocations and crisis in order to enhance the role of the U.N. They will do this because they regard the U.N. as a stepping stone to a future World Government."

Montgomery points to the Stimson Center, a liberal think tank in D.C. that proposed a federation of nations put all the world's military power into the hands of the U.N. (NWG). With this military power, no nation, including the U.S., could oppose its policies, no matter how objectionable they were. Remember that Henry Stimson was Secretary of War for FDR and an advocate of sacrificing Pearl Harbor to the Japanese to get into World War II.

On September 6, 2000, President Clinton supported the disarming of the American military and the creation of the New World Government army. It will be the foundation of the U.N. army, called the Rapid Reaction Force. Ratification of the U.N. Reform Treaty would give many of the powers now provided by our Constitution to the United Nations. And if two-thirds of the members agreed to increase the obligations of membership, such an increase would become binding on all nations, even those who opposed such an expansion of powers. There are no provisions in the U.N. Charter for termination of membership.

If you go to their web site www.un.org/millennium/sg/report/index, you will see that in the full report they have omitted freedom of religion and speech, but still include freedom from want, and freedom from fear, as chapters three and four. This sentence from the first chapter is rather telling: "Globalization offers great opportunities, but at present its benefits are very unevenly distributed while its costs are borne by all." It sounds like Marxist Global Speak. And you will notice that the beginning of the chapter starts with *We The Peoples of the United Nations*. Willi Munzenberg couldn't have said it better!

No country has ever been able to eliminate the fear and want of their citizens, Yet America is supposed to consider discarding our Constitution in favor of a U.N. that is morally corrupt. For the last several years Bill

Clinton has been campaigning to replace Kofi Annan when his term expires in 2006. Clinton's political genius may be second only to that of FDR, but his character is a disgrace. The only reason Hillary has stayed with him is that she hopes to ride his coattails to the White House.

Gary Aldrich, author of *Unlimited Access* and an FBI agent for more than 30 years, described the Clinton staffers he had contact with as an organization that had almost no regard for honesty and integrity. He details the cover-up of the Vince Foster suicide (Vince was Hillary's former lover) and the Travel Gate episode as nothing short of scandalous. The coronation of Bill Clinton as the head of the U.N. is unthinkable!

And though I agree that the conservatives are more likely to support individual liberty than are the liberals, when power is at stake all bets are off. President Bush continues to talk in sound bites to the American people, demeaning our intelligence as he secretly serves up America to the Global Elite. The fate of the American people still rests in our hands, but for how long? We need to educate ourselves, and our children, for it is their future that is at stake. We have to examine the issues carefully and not be fooled by unattainable goals such as world peace and freedom from want and fear. We cannot believe in an idealistic bumper sticker mentality based on delusional thinking.

For there can be no doubt that we are fighting for the very survival of this great Republic. The 21st century will be marked by failed states, such as we are witnessing in Africa and the Middle East, where loyalty is transferred to ethnic and religious groups, tribes, localities, and ideologies. These failed states are likely to become centers of increased terror and chaos. If we are to survive this war of chaos, William Lind, in his previously mentioned article, points out that we need two things: an open political system and a unified culture. What we have right now, he says, is a closed political system dominated by a single political party. In *Stealing Elections*, John Fund describes how the two parties are in collusion when it comes to the national debates, how they keep the

American people from knowing the real truth. *Our political system has been perverted so that it serves the interests of the politicians instead of the people.*

Lind claims that the first step is to end the de facto policy of open immigration. We have to close the borders immediately. However, this becomes extremely difficult when groups like the American Civil Liberties Union get involved, for they are another of the many groups used by the Global Elite to confuse and divide the American people. Although they have an image as a defender of liberty, that is far from the truth.

The current Executive Director of the ACLU, Anthony Romero, is a member of the CFR, who had previously been in charge of the Ford Foundation's grant program.   Romero spent $90 million of Foundation money putting out *crisis* messages used to scare the public into accepting bigger government, including laws like the Patriot Act. (Although the ACLU has come out against the Patriot Act, they have done almost nothing in the court system to challenge it. Their protests sound like Willi Munzenberg double-speak). The Ford Foundation has funded studies and groups that promote crisis mentality on issues such as population growth and environmental conservation. The Foundation is a major source of funding for MALDEF, La Raza, and other Hispanic separatist groups that add to the turmoil in states such as Texas and California. Although not likely to succeed, these groups help to fan the flames of fear and dread, making the public believe that only a bigger, more powerful government can save us.

By taking on cases that are involved in removing the word God from anything associated with government, the ACLU has become an obstructionist force in society seeking to define the narrow parameters of politically acceptable groupthink. This is another example of destroying the fabric of society from within, using the rights of a few as a club to obstruct other's right of free speech. Again, this is similar to what Hitler wanted to do in the early stages: remove God from society, as described in *Mein Kampf.*

It is important that we adopt a defensive, rather than an offensive, military strategy. If we are not fighting wars all over the world, we can use our resources to rebuild our schools and infrastructure. The world will always be a dangerous place, but we should build and maintain our system of defense such that any nation would be foolish to even consider attacking us. The next step is to reform our political system. Lind suggests that we also reinstate term limits, make more use of ballot initiatives, and restrain the Judiciary from legislating.

Those who insist that the globalization of the world cannot be stopped might be right. But that does not mean we have to surrender our liberties to the politicians of global groupthink. In fact, only by resisting this propaganda can we hold on to the illustrious American Dream that is the heritage of our Founding Fathers. Otherwise, our politicians are going to auction it off to the highest bidder.

25

THE URGE TO SAVE HUMANITY IS ALMOST ALWAYS A FALSE FACE FOR THE URGE TO RULE IT

H.L. Mencken

At this point it appears obvious that history can teach us several things about war. First and foremost: if our politicians are going to get the American people behind any war effort, they will have to lie. But they are good at that.

Most recently, we can blame the lack of weapons of mass destruction on our intelligence agencies. George Tenet was the sacrificial goat this time around, though in December, 2004, President Bush awarded him with the Presidential Medal of Freedom, the nation's highest civilian award. Again, it seems Bush is talking out of both sides of his mouth. Was Tenet responsible for bad intelligence or wasn't he? Or was this just the reward for falling on his sword?

Each time there has been a military engagement the government has expanded its role and size militarily, with very little downsizing once the conflict was over. Remember, the thing that impressed FDR the most about World War I was the incredible expansion of governmental power and the increased ability to dictate to the American public.

The Patriot Act was supposed to be a temporary necessity to catch the bad guys among us who wanted to kill the American Dream. The only problem was that our government didn't take the necessary steps to protect us, such as securing the border and enforcing the laws. With each conflict the liberties of America are diminished.

The Democrats don't seem to mind all that much, being the big government advocates that they are. For the longer the war in Iraq drags on, the more certain they are of regaining the White House in 2008. And a larger government will only mean more authority for Hillary to socialize us with the radical ideas from her days at Wellesley College and Yale Law School. She can continue to glorify the welfare-warfare state while just dispensing with the Mexican border altogether. That should solidify her base with the Latino vote.

Thomas P.M. Barnett has presented what may be the ideal format for the Right's vision of a New World Order, in *The Pentagon's New Map*. This new approach to warfare is so slick it makes me think FDR has reincarnated as Mr. Barnett. As he sees it, the 1990s were a time of confusion and chaos for the U.S. military, which fought in more crisis-response conflicts such as Haiti, Somalis, and Kosovo, than in any previous decade. His backhanded compliment to Bill Clinton was that he bought a new military yet continued to fight with the old one.

Barnett has created a new global government with its own national security lexicon that is hitting home runs with the Pentagon and the military. He has neatly divided the world into two groups: the Core, which has connectivity, and the Gap, which doesn't have or doesn't want connectivity. Those who have or desire connectivity are playing by the new *Rule Set* that worships globalization and thinks everyone should adopt this new ideology. Those who don't favor globalization reject connectivity and the cultural content flow and are the bad actors. They represent the areas that are going to be hot spots filled with malcontents.

Barnett's new map is designed to eradicate the bad actors and gives the Pentagon a new *Rule Set* by which to police the globe. His vision is based on the premise that the U.S. military is the most formidable and powerful the world has ever known, and he praises the absolutely fantastic job they did of winning the war in Iraq. The problem was that we lost the peace in Iraq, which our military was never intended to safeguard.

The answer, according to Barnett, is to maintain two international forces. The first force would be known as the *kick down the door* brigade, and those that followed, the second force, would be the *humanitarian peacekeeping* brigade. He believes that we should have put 200,000 more boots on the ground in Iraq, boots that specialize in peacekeeping. Then we would leave them there for as long as it takes to completely stabilize the situation while pulling out the fighting force. Barnett believes that this would have made Iraq a winner all the way around. The peacekeeping force would be primarily non-American men and women of color, because they would blend in better and might engender less resistance. This would allow us to extract the initial fighting units.

Barnett's global government has a military with two divisions, each broken up into three groups. Group A of the *kick down the door* division would function like a Grand Jury and hand down indictments. The B group would be the Executive branch running the show, and the C group would be the fighting soldiers. In the *humanitarian peacekeeping* division, the X team would be the occupation forces, the Y team would be something akin to the International Monetary Fund that provides the financing, and the Z team would be the international criminal court.

Here is how it would all fit together: Osama bin Laden would start to make threats, as he did prior to 9/11, and Group A would get together and decide whether it met what candidate Kerry called a global test. If it did, then they would hand down an indictment to Group B, and a *kick down the door* response by Group C would follow. After the battle was won, the *humanitarian peacekeeping* division would send in their troops and stability would eventually be realized. Or Osama might actually commit an act of terror, such as 9/11, which is called a *System Perturbance,* which would also trigger a *kick down the door* response, etc.

The reason Bush failed in attracting more international support was that he told our allies that since they hadn't participated in the fight, they weren't going to be allowed to share in the spoils. Barnett says his system wouldn't make such a mistake, because it would be comprised of international members right from the start. The whole motivation behind his ideology would be to increase everybody's *Broadband Network Connectivity*, meaning the other nations' investment in the global collective.

It is interesting that Barnett almost never makes reference to the United Nations or their Rapid Response Force, which I believe is his way of being politic. Barnett realizes that with all the scandals in the U.N. right now, he couldn't call this new organization by its real name. And he saw the fear of the American people when they suspected that candidate Kerry might cede the right to defend the United States to the U.N. Being a member of the U.S. Naval War College, Barnett knows how to play politics.

It is also interesting to note that Barnett believes that the Nixon plan to use Iran as the foundation for stability in the Middle East was the right one. But he blames the former Shah for trying to modernize too quickly. He conveniently ignores the Shah's 25-year reign of terror, torture, and murder that motivated the Iranian revolt in the first place.

But there is another fault with the Barnett plan. It is common for resistance to die down for months or even years before a guerrilla attack is mounted. Time is on their side as they fade into the background and await their opportunity. The December 2004 attack on a mess tent in Mosul by a group of terrorists pinpoints a problem particular to the

Muslim world. The group that claimed responsibility for killing 22 American soldiers while they ate identified itself as Ansar al Sunnah, and they released a video of the attack on an Internet site. In it they even specified lunchtime as the hour at which they bombed the *Crusaders*. For much of the Muslim world this is a holy war, and they see the West as a part of the *Crusades*. If they are continually killing their own people in Iraq, a group of humanitarians with brown skin is not going to stop their struggle. And they do not appear to lack *Connectivity*.

FDR would have a field day selling Barnett's plan, for it incorporates his Four Freedoms under the simple slogan of *increasing bandwidth* to give the world more economic and social stability. And his idea of big government has reached the global proportions he envisioned for himself. Barnett's plan does recognize that the world may never become a paradise on earth, which is what FDR was trying to sell—or maybe that was just part of the propaganda? Barnett's plan divides the world in two, with the good guys (the United Nations) promoting *bandwidth connectivity* (globalization) and the bad actors (mostly Muslims) constantly trying to create *system perturbances* (disconnecting bandwidth).

Make no mistake about it, Thomas P.M. Barnett is the first golden boy of the 21st century, for he has given the military/industrial complex a vision so compelling, not to mention self-serving, that it is already being swallowed in big gulps. He has given three presentations a week over the last year to many of the decision makers in the U.S. military and around the world. He is the self-described Mick Jagger of a newly emerging paradigm for the New World Order, and the Pentagon wants him to sing his song for every one-star general in our military.

Barnett's Gap area is centered in the Middle East and includes all of Africa and much of southeast and southwest Asia. He acknowledges that the Muslims have shown the will to fight indefinitely. But he is convinced that global government with a *kick down the door* and a *humanitarian peacekeeping* force will be victorious wherever the Gap rears its ugly head.

Barnett does recognize the significance of oil, and he clearly spells out that the world, especially China, Japan, and Korea, will have a desperate need for that energy in the next few decades. So besides persuading Iran to become a good guy that wants connectivity, he states the need to get rid of Kim in the North and reunite Korea. And the beauty of this, as he sees it, is that he is not attaching the success of his plan to creating democracies, which everyone but Bush and his inner circle agrees is totally untenable. He is simply promoting stability, which will benefit all the multinationals. We know their only goal is to enhance their profit margins.

Barnett foresees American servicemen and women stationed on Spartan-style military bases that will spring up all around the globe. His video presentation is rather seductive for those who base their careers on power. And yet Barnett claims that the death of any American soldier breaks his heart! He says he is certain his global government will minimize deaths, because the *kick down the door* force is what the U.S. does best.

On his video he says the only question that Congressmen will ask is, "*Can you build it in my home state?*" Barnett is convinced that his new plan will eliminate the need for borders, that religious differences will cease to be an issue, and that we will end all war as we knew it in the twentieth century.

This Brave New World the Pentagon adores will be much loved by other nations who want what America has enjoyed for two hundred years. The U.N. was supposed to eliminate wars like Korea, Vietnam and Kosovo, but the U.N. supporters blame this failure on the Cold War and believe the situation can be remedied by bringing in the right person. Eager for power, the U.N. wants to dismiss the last 15 years of confusion, corruption, and decay.

There can be very little doubt that *The Pentagon's New Map* is nothing short of the neoconservatives' wildest and most exhilarating wet dream. The *kick down the door* mentality appeals to the Right, while the *humanitarian peacekeeping* mission appeals to the Left. So the choice will be between someone like Bush, or the alternative, which is Hillary. I understand that she is now stating that God is an important force in her life. It sounds as if she is already campaigning for the 2008 Presidential election.

On paper, and even in the video presentation, Barnett does make it sound rather like the utopian answer for Internet lovers who can never get enough bandwidth. Certainly his title, U.S. Naval War College Senior Strategic Researcher, is impressive. And the fact that a whole new language has been coined for the military, putting them ahead of the curve for once, might make the idea of a global police force sound sexy.

Barnett speaks very little about money, but his stand-up comedy routine and his powers of persuasion allow him to gloss over the price. I am firmly convinced that this plan, or something very similar to it, has already been privately agreed to by the Puppet Masters. The real question is, how much will it cost the American people? That is what we will look at in the next chapter.

PART V

These United States of America can never be destroyed...
from forces outside its borders. If America falls, it will fall
from within. Brought down by apathy. When good people do
nothing, anarchy reigns.

We the people are the rightful masters of Congress and
the courts, not to overthrow the Constitution, but to overthrow
men who would pervert the Constitution.

— Abraham Lincoln

26

THE LAWS OF NATURE AND NATURE'S GOD

The Pentagon's New Map will have grave consequences for all Americans, as it will represent the end of America, as we know it. The effort to win world support and financing for this global government will necessitate that we surrender many of our freedoms to the New World Order. Our liberties will be sacrificed for the welfare of greater connectivity to places like China, India, Europe, Russia, etc. Their way of life may not change much, but ours will disappear forever.

As in any new marriage, the honeymoon will be rather carefree. But as the bloom wears off the rose and the Americas are no longer separate, our cities will be overrun with those from Latin America looking to find better paying jobs. This will displace all but those with high technology skills, until our hourly wage is at equilibrium with that of China and India. We will become the second-class citizens.

This New World Order has been in the works for many decades now. William F. Jasper does an excellent job of showing how the Global Elite are accomplishing their goal of one government under the United Nations in his book, *Global Tyranny... Step By Step*. He quotes Edith Kermit Roosevelt (Theodore Roosevelt's granddaughter): "What is the Establishment's viewpoint? Through the Roosevelt, Truman, Eisenhower, and Kennedy administrations its ideology is constant: that the best way to fight Communism is by a One-World Socialist state governed by the 'experts' like themselves."

Some people in our society have been warning about this welfare-warfare state for decades, but the Global Elite have been able mold the opinion of the masses by controlling the media and ridiculing those who have been trying to warn us. These secret conspirators have survived since the Crusades by being astute students of history and masters of the media, brutally efficient in carrying out their agenda. Their goal is in sight.

Homogeneity will be the rule, and cultural differences will not be tolerated, for they will breed discord. Several hundred million people will be insignificant in the face of six billion. Right now, because we honor a state's right to sanction gay marriage, it is accepted that if Massachusetts, California, or any other state wishes to allow gay marriage, it can do so as long as it does not require federal taxpayers to contribute to their union in the form of Social Security benefits, etc. Likewise, the right of a woman to choose abortion may never be denied in California or many other states, because our Constitution guarantees that right to those states that so choose.

Our freedom of religion and to speak out against tyranny is also guaranteed, but already the Global Elite is tampering with those rights. One example is hate speech. I personally detest hearing someone say he hates another person or group, but it should not be a crime to express such an emotion, because it is a short step from there to having the Global Elite make it a crime to criticize the U.N.—or, God forbid, to say one hates the U.N.

The next step will be to monitor what we think. If we surrender our Constitutional protections to this New World Order, none of us will be safe. The inalienable rights we take for granted right now could easily be denied. For with Americans busy trying to earn a living and highly specialized *kick down the door* troops stationed in Norway or Malaysia, or Tijuana, our liberties will be in serious jeopardy!

Probably the first group of people to defect will be our politicians, for they will be falling all over themselves to land lifetime appointments to the New World Order, whether it be called the United Nations or something else. By simply putting a new face at the head of the U.N., be it Clinton, Powell, Kissinger, or George Soros, the Global Elite won't have to reinvent the wheel—just polish the image a bit.

At first much of our current military will follow their leaders, until they realize they have been duped. Right now American soldiers are willing to sacrifice their lives in Iraq because they are being told that spreading democracy in the Middle East will make America safer from terrorist attacks. But they will soon realize that we cannot force freedom and democracy on the Middle East, or anywhere else for that matter. They will understand that elections don't create democracies. Democracies create elections. They will soon see that they are giving their lives so that the monolithic mentality of Big Brother can build a new McDonald's franchise in the Sudan. They will know in their hearts that once we surrender the authority of our Constitution we will never get it back. The New World Order will not tolerate anyone who challenges its authority.

At this time it is imperative that we obey the laws and come together as Americans with our common heritage to halt the progress of the Global Elite. It is essential that we spread the word to all of our friends and family, warn them of the impending danger, and work together to change the system. We do not want to break the laws or get violent, and we want to avoid the tragedies of Ruby Ridge and Waco, Texas. But the more time that passes, the more sophisticated their technology becomes, the more difficult will be our challenge. And those who now speak of the Constitution as antiquated and irrelevant may regret that they didn't defend it when they had the chance.

The cultural elite that graduated from Yale Law School and the like, who have given us so much political correctness that we can't tell right from wrong, who have suffocated us with so many laws that we can't breathe and so mush regulation that we have forgotten common sense, might remember something Cicero once said: *the more laws you have, the less justice there is.* More and more people are going to start asking, *Whatever Happened to Justice?* And those who can find that little treasure by Richard Maybury are going to dig it out and dust it off, and then they will realize what they have lost!

For you see, the American Dream wasn't an idea born of conscious consideration. It came about as a by-product of honesty, integrity, hard work, and the desire for liberty from oppression. It was so incredibly successful that it gave birth to the greatest civilization the world has ever known. But slowly, starting early in the 1900s, the ideology of socialism crossed the Atlantic and infected our institutions. This disease was hastened along by FDR in the New Deal, until it was ingrained in our psyche and had tightened its grip on our very soul. Sweating out this toxic waste will be painful and difficult. The Global Elite will fight us every step of the way, and this will most assuredly be the toughest battle we have ever fought.

Today this global conglomerate is trying to convince us that we can export the American Dream, via the United Nations, to the world. President Bush screams it every time he claims that by spreading democracy we are becoming safer. This dream that some want so much to believe in is a cancerous nightmare that is devouring our strength and vitality with each passing day. Obviously, Bush is delusional, and that is part of the problem. The American Dream cannot be bought, sold, or given away. The American Dream has to be earned, it has to be fought for, it has to be won.

During the twentieth century the Global Elite used fear of Nazism and then of Communism to motivate us to surrender our liberties. Our leaders lied, convincing us that we had to win it *over there*, wherever "there" was. Now that the Berlin wall has fallen, they are trying to motivate us by appealing to our generous and idealistic side, hoping we won't see how they have manipulated us. All the while our leaders, including FDR, Truman, Johnson, Nixon, Bush, and Clinton have been stealing from us, looking us right in the face and lying. Only they haven't called it thievery, they've called it entitlement, empowerment, and anything else that sounded good, just so long as they could play God.

That's why they fight so hard to eliminate God from our vocabulary. As I said earlier, we all pray to the same God—Christian, Jew, Hindu, or Muslim. The rest is interpretation. I won't force my God on you if you won't force your God on me. When I say God I don't meant Christ, the Bible, or Buddha. That's why our Founding Fathers spoke of *the Laws of Nature and Nature's God*. Their wisdom is even more profound today!

Jeanette Rankin was the first woman ever elected to Congress, and she voted no to World War I because, as she put it, "I knew that none of the idealistic hopes would be carried out and I was aware of the falseness of much of the propaganda." Her vote was not popular, and she was not reelected. In fact, it was taught that she voted no because she was a woman, and women can't be expected to have the same courage as men. The message was that women couldn't be trusted to make important decisions.

After Pearl Harbor, as a Senator, she was the only member of Congress to vote against entering World War II. That took an incredible amount of courage, and was so unpopular she needed protection from an angry public. Yet she knew the history of FDR and she did not trust him; she saw through the façade that captivated so many Americans. Later in her life she protested against the Vietnam War. She is a true American hero. How different this world would be if we had heeded her wisdom! You can google her for her biography.

I am convinced that preventing *The Pentagon's New Map* from becoming a reality will be exceedingly difficult, for it is being championed by those on both the Left and the Right. The only possibility is for the American people to unite, to put aside our minor differences, and to realize that if we sacrifice our Constitution to the global collective, we are giving up the greatest form of government the world has ever known. We are sacrificing the American Dream, and the dark days of despair will soon descend upon the future of all our children.

27

DESTROYING A NATION FROM WITHIN

There have been secret organizations since the time of Pythagoras, in which information was never written down but only passed on to initiates by word of mouth. Certainly the Catholic Church has had its share of secrets, even though it is not an underground organization. To survive in such a devious time as the Dark Ages, when the kings and the Church were a law unto themselves, must have required tremendous skill, discipline, cunning, and patience.

The Knights Templar managed to escape that first unlucky Friday the thirteenth, 1307, and even flourish. They out-lasted the cutthroat kings and outwitted the Catholic Church. Perhaps at times they saw fit to form temporary alliances with the Church, for in a way they make for the perfect dialectic: a secret society of religiosity versus a secret society of pirates and plunderers, competing for the soul of Everyman, and at a handsome profit.

The Order, the Illuminati, the Bilderbergs, and their compatriot groups have been extremely influential in determining the course of events in America and abroad for many centuries. If the United States is the last bastion of defense standing in the way of a New World Order, what would it take to bring down the United States from within?

The end game would be the final implementation of a plan to have the government become our Global God, with all individuals conditioned to the premise that it is their role to serve the state, which would be run by the members of these secret societies or their proxies. It would be interesting to see if this Global Elite would be so concerned with women's rights once they have achieved their objective of global domination. Or would they prefer to have them perform in more traditional roles, roles in which their minds don't matter?

It has to be clearly understood that to these secret societies, which are exclusively male, all people and governments outside their groups are simply pawns to be manipulated for their own gain. After all, once they gain control of all of the power, the Hegelian clash of opposites would not be nearly so necessary. Yet if they were really smart, which they certainly appear to be, they would continue to stimulate minor conflicts within the various cultures around the world for several reasons: first, it would keep the masses happy, as they would have something to argue about and fight over, and most people love a good fight; second, after playing God for all of these centuries, I should think that it would be rather dull not to keep the game going just for the fun of it. Very few people stop playing a game once they have mastered it. And finally, they would want to keep their military unit sharp.

The Global Elite have degraded the educational system of America, using it to socialize the child to become a productive member of the Hegelian state. Sutton's book *America's Secret Establishment* presents detailed and alarming information on how this was accomplished. They have used every possible issue to fragment American society, from gun control and God to gay rights, the environment, and the concept of marriage. Their message has been pounding us 24/7 through the media for decades. They preach diversity as their newest mantra, while the borders have been abandoned, the currency has been debased for so long it is nearing catastrophic levels, and the rights of the individual are quickly disappearing. It is almost to the point that the American personality can best be described as schizophrenic.

These secret groups have not only learned from history, they have passed down their knowledge from generation to generation such that they have molded the present and are almost able to predict the future, or at least to know which way the wind will blow and profit from it. As Americans we think 50 years is a long time, but to them 50 years is the bottom of the first inning, just enough time to get warmed up. They already have such enormous power and wealth that they can live in luxury as they wage their war for global domination.

Some might say it would be impossible for a group of men to allow what the Nazis did just because it was profitable and they could. It is interesting that Theodore Roosevelt, a member of the Masons, and known for his trust-busting activities, is on record as being a racist. Sora quotes on page 270, in *Secret Societies of America's Elite*: "I wish very much that the wrong people could be prevented from breeding...." While he ranted about the unwashed masses, the Eugenics Records Office (ERO) was created and funded by John D. Rockefeller, whose General Education Board was originally funded by groups close to the Order of Skull and Bones, the Carnegie Institute, George Eastman, and the widow of E.H. Harriman (of Brown Brothers, Harriman, and father to Averill of the Order, class of 1913).

The ERO singled out undesirable traits such as alcoholism and an inordinate love of the sea, and then sought to sterilize those who exhibited them. The movement grew in America and was adopted by Nazi Germany, which then took it to its ultimate expression. There is no accounting for the possibility of genetic malfunction within the Order itself. There have been rather a lot of intermarriages within the families that make up this group, with names such as Whitney, Phelps, Perkins, Norton, and Putnam used as middle (maternal) names. We will probably never know how this interbreeding has affected their gene pool.

As we have seen, in almost every war one of the casualties is the surrender of more personal liberty. It was James Madison who stridently warned that war was the primary means by which a President expands his power at the expense of individual freedom, as Bush is now demonstrating. Propaganda (WMD) was used to take fear to hysterical heights as personal freedoms were lost, while the door (our borders) was left open for terrorists.

One might ask: if the Order and its sister organizations were to reach their goal of globalization, which form of government will they prefer, socialism or free enterprise? My guess is that it will be a totalitarian regime disguised as a democracy. Health care will be socialized and individuals will lose the ability to choose their health care provider, as the doctors will be spread over a larger portion of the globe. The quality of service will be substantially less than we are used to, although a mid-level management group might get better service, and of course the elite will avail themselves of the best doctors money can buy.

The whole purpose of these nefarious secret groups from the very beginning has been to create wealth for themselves through any means possible. Early on, they mastered banking and commerce while evading the taxes of the kings. They have created wars, revolutions, depressions, and inflation to topple governments for profit. They bought large media conglomerates to entertain and numb the youth and much of the adult population while still making a profit. And they have developed cheap and effective pharmaceuticals to ease our increased tendencies towards psychosis and schizophrenia as the foundations of society crumble all around us. And of course it all facilitates the continued development of the intended New World Order. The remaining revolutionary few will have to be dealt with in the harshest way possible.

The use of communism/socialism was nothing more than a ruse, a tactical ploy used in a dialectical fashion to rally the Russians who had suffered harshly under the Czars, or the liberals in America with their dreams of utopia and aspirations for world peace. But when the mask comes off you will see the grim face of a dictator comparable to Hitler and Stalin. If you are not that familiar with a totalitarian society, it would be worth your time to rent the video of a Russian film made in the early 1990s called *Burnt By the Sun*. It is a chilling tale that may be coming to a town near you in the near future.

The New World Government religion might tend toward a watered-down version of Unitarian teachings. It is interesting to note that the Unitarian church was co-founded by William Taft's father, Alphonso Taft, who also co-founded the Order of Skull and Bones. Alphonso Taft was Secretary of War in 1876. Several members of the Order held this position, which was renamed the Secretary of Defense, into the 1950s. William Taft was president of the Unitarian Association in his time. This comes from Constance Cumbey, whose book *The Hidden Dangers of the Rainbow* links Hitler to the New Age movement.

Listen to what President Woodrow Wilson had to say, as quoted by Carroll Quigley in his book *Tragedy and Hope*: "Some of the biggest men in the U.S. in the fields of commerce and manufacturing know that there is a power so complete, so subtle, so pervasive that they had better not speak above their breath when they speak in condemnation of it." This was the man who got us into World War I at the very end of the conflict, and for no good reason. What did Wilson know that he was so afraid of that he wouldn't name it?

It was Bill Clinton's World Government mentor, Carroll Quigley, who said that the movement for a New World Government was too far along to stop. Although he died in 1977, even then he felt that the power of the Global Elite was already too great to resist. However, he admitted that they did fear the average citizen, for that is the source of all their power and wealth. By means of deception and manipulation the secret members of the elite have managed to get the average citizens to support its subversive goals.

Sutton received much of the documentation for *America's Secret Establishment*, first published in 1983, from a secret source too afraid to make his identity known. He identifies every member of the Order of Skill and Bones from 1833 (with one exception) through 1985. The legal name for the Order is The Russell Trust, and some of the original documents for this organization are at Yale University. Since the publication of its first volume of *The Sterling Library* at Yale, they have refused to allow researchers access to The Russell Trust papers.

One of the first things we have to realize is the value and importance of the family. Breaking up the family has been at the heart of these secret organizations for decades. From the earliest of civilizations, the family has been the bedrock of our culture, the foundation of our future. The Global Elite has been waging a mighty war against the family for a long time. The work of Hillary Clinton that I mentioned earlier is just one example of many assaults that have been made over many decades. By destroying the fabric of the family, by finding fault with the parental system, the Global Elite make it easier to promote the rationalization that children should be raised by the state. The closer they get to this goal, the sooner they will be able to claim their victory.

We must take back the control of our children's education and teach them to think critically. We must demand that American history be taught, even if we have to resort to more home schooling. It will be almost impossible to get Congress to deal with this problem, so it will have to be done on a state-by-state basis.

We have to put America first in so many areas that it will be a long and difficult struggle. One of the best ways to destroy a nation is to debase the currency, and one of the best ways to debase a currency is through inflation, which is exactly what has been happening in a big way since the House of Morgan forced the Bretton Woods agreement on us. Yet George Soros and our politicians never mention this. Is it a coincidence?

Maintaining open borders invites the Mexican invasion. The mass inflows are destroying our educational system, our history, our culture, and ultimately our liberty. If the new and illegal immigrants are not concerned with assimilating into our culture, if they do not care to understand what makes this country great, then they will not know why they should work to protect the Declaration of Independence or the Constitution. They will be happy to do anything they are told so long as the Global Elite will let them stay in America. But the American Dream will have disappeared. So it should be obvious why neither Kerry nor Bush, both members of the Order, would come out in support of enforcing our laws and securing the border during the 2004 election.

We have to stay out of foreign wars unless they are absolutely essential to our national defense, for they kill off our best and brightest young Americans, increasing both inflation and our federal deficit.

Our first priority, after educating the young minds that are the future, is to make certain that we can protect the homeland against every invader, and that we can destroy whatever enemy appears at our door. Economic times may get tough, for we have given this Global Elite the keys to our safe, and they will do everything in their considerable power to wreak havoc on those of us who would stand and challenge their authority.

I will discuss several specific strategies in the last chapter.

28

THERE COMES A TIME WHEN SILENCE IS BETRAYAL

Martin Luther King Jr.

I have tried to outline for you the process by which I came to understand that the American Dream, indeed the American way of life, is in serious jeopardy. It is a sad and shocking story that will be hard for many people to comprehend. The facts are laid out all around us, but they are blurred by the confusion and chaos of our fast-paced, schizophrenic society, and the media is working overtime to obscure the truth. If I were to tell you that there is an easy solution to the many problems I have outlined here I would be lying. But in some ways the solution is quite simple.

There are powerful forces working in the shadows of our government who appear to be pillars of society, but are in fact masters of disguise and practiced in the art of deception. I will tell you up front that the plan to defeat them is simple, but the way will be hard and painful, for they have many tools at their disposal. The have power and untold riches, and all we have is the truth. Our victory could mean the end of their Crusade for global domination, or at least an uncomfortable delay. They have been pursuing their goal of world conquest for many a century, against kings, monarchs, and popes, so we cannot expect it to be easy.

But there is a joy in the truth that is so contagious, so liberating, that we can defeat them and their paparazzi of propaganda if we work together. In fact we have to, because the alternative will be so much worse it will cause our children and future generations unbearable suffering. Each one of us in our daily lives will have the opportunity to recognize the truth, to be able to tell the glitter from the gold. We have to begin now, and we have to tell all of our friends and loved ones and explain that the future of America rests on our shoulders.

The Declaration of Independence, the United States Constitution, and the Bill of Rights are the banners of liberation and freedom that speak our truth. Our mission will be to try and make every citizen, and especially every politician of this nation, understand that these documents are the key to our survival. For decades our enemies have posed as our friends as they have tried to dismantle these three cornerstones of our Republic. But they have forgotten that the fourth cornerstone is a living and breathing human being who treasures the American Dream and cannot live without it.

In the last hundred years we have lost hundreds of thousands of our bravest soldiers as they laid their lives down on the battlefield to preserve the liberty of other nations. Today we are fighting a new kind of war, a revolution of words and ideas that were first given breath in 1776, and each of us is heir to that legacy. Who will be the next George Washington, Thomas Jefferson, or Abraham Lincoln? The freedoms they fought for are in danger of being taken from us without a shot being fired. That is how clever, how sophisticated, how determined and dangerous is the enemy we now face.

If I had to make a guess, here is how I see the Global Elite making their final assault on American Liberty. It will be in the form of some kind of extremely contagious disease. It will be thrust down upon us in secret and will necessitate the declaration of a state of emergency. This will allow the military police to swoop down upon those who would seek to expose the Global Elite and their minions to the light of truth. Those who work to preserve justice and individual liberty will be condemned and taken away, falsely accused of spreading a plague among society. These people will never be seen or heard from again, and after several weeks and many deaths the all clear will be sounded.

I hope that I am wrong and that it never comes to this, but the longer we wait before taking nonviolent action, the stronger they become. We have to use our vote and all the legal means at our disposal. There are millions of us, and only a few of them. But don't underestimate their power and influence. They haven't survived since the Crusades without being extremely clever and brutal.

So this is a call to arms, but not those of powder and steel. This is a clarion call to your heart, to your essence as Soul, to all that you hold precious in this world that is based on your God-given rights under the United States Constitution. Most often our victories will be quiet ones when no one else is around, when the light goes on and you realize that some magazine ad or television commercial is singing its siren song. Or some slick politician will be trying to convince you that the government is your friend and needs just a little more control over your financial well being. Or when you realize that the pretty face on TV was bought and paid for by the enemy, not to pick your pocket, but to pick your mind.

This is what the thought police have been after for so long: your mind. And once they have that, they believe they can bargain for you heart and soul as well. The issues that confront us on a daily basis can be confusing to the point that it may seem easier to subscribe to the groupthink spouted by the media and so many of our politicians. But this is a bargain with the devil. He will promise you an easier life filled with sweet dreams, only to leave you empty and hollow and sick to your stomach. The thought police are selling drugs of the most potent kind, but the intoxication is temporary, and the freedoms lost could take a lifetime of struggle to get back.

It is incredibly disheartening to know that most of our leaders are in on the scam. We pay them comfortable salaries and give them generous retirement and health care benefits, but still the system works against us. It is clear that business as usual is not working. So I am going to propose a different approach to politics and the taking back of our government.

Over the years there have been those who have tried to establish a third party, or at least an independent alternative to politics as usual. But a third party candidate, being attacked by both the liberal and conservative party, appears to be an impossible alternative. As we have seen, the two-party system has a vested interest in maintaining the status quo.

If you have ever been involved in an intervention to get a family member or loved one off of drugs or alcohol, you know how difficult it can be. Well, that is what we are facing here. I agree that there are some in Washington who have been able to maintain their integrity, but they are a small minority. When confronted by multinational corporations willing to pay them millions of dollars in campaign contributions that would be called bribes in many countries, most of them will become corrupted. As Kissinger (CFR, BB, TC) has pointed out, power is the ultimate aphrodisiac.

To succeed in this intervention, we will have to come together as a nation. We will need to put aside our minor differences, so that we can focus our energy on effecting the most important changes first. I would like to propose a *Political Action Committee For The People*, a political organization based on issues instead of candidates. Rather than trying to find the perfect candidate who can speak to the many and diverse issues that face us today, I am suggesting that we, as Americans, try and focus on the most critical issues first, that we husband our political strength—our vote—and force Congress and the President to represent us.

Each person or family has certain issues they feel are most critical, whether it be the war on terror, immigration and the open borders, the budget deficit, or election reform. My suggestion is that we decide what our priorities are, and then work toward solving the most important problems facing America, not using the political party method, but by focusing on individual issues. I believe that if a significant portion of Americans will register to vote as *Independents*, and put their weight behind specific issues rather than hoping that the candidates will keep their promises, we can get the politicians to listen to us.

If 15 to 20% of the voting population registered as *Independent Voters* for the 2006 election, our political force would be staggering. The sound bites and spin-doctors would become irrelevant, because the politicians would have to listen to us, the voters, and hear what is important to us. Then they would have to talk intelligently about the real issues facing the nation. Having a large base of *Independent voters* will confuse them, as the polls they love so much will not be as effective.

The power of the Internet allows us to become voters who are aligned behind specific problems. The politicians will have to deal with us as intelligent voters with serious demands, and they will have to come down off of their power perches and listen to us, and then act responsibly. In the 2004 election about five percent made the difference. If we could convince 10% to register as *Independent voters* we would be a force that would have to be recognized and listened to.

We are not a dictatorship, and I hope we will never walk in lockstep, but unless we stand up and make our voice heard, unless we take back our vote and make it count, the politicians will continue to treat us as they have been. I am tired of it, and I hope you feel the same way. When I hear that 95% of the American people do not believe that illegal aliens are entitled to the same freedoms as citizens under the Constitution of the United States, and yet the politicians ignore this because MALDEF has large corporations paying their bills, I am disgusted.

Our politicians have been selling us down the river to the highest bidder, and our schools are broken. We pay more for health care than any other country and yet have the shortest life span in the western world, and many of our hospitals are nearly bankrupt. Our prisons in the southwestern states are overflowing with illegal aliens because the federal government is not enforcing the law and securing our borders, and Mexican gangs are now selling young girls into the sex/slave industry. Our brave young soldiers are dying for oil in a land that will never be free from the hatred of radical terrorists, and we have to end the vicious cycle that makes America the world's policeman. The U.N. is a tool of the Global Elite that is committed to poisoning the liberties upon which America was founded, the liberties that we cannon live without. Our budget deficit is about to crush us, yet the politicians keep spending our money to get them re-elected. And most of all I am sickened that the Global Elite has such disdain for the American people.

With this in mind, I am starting an Internet site dedicated to maintaining our Constitutional freedoms. Each person who becomes an American Eagle Member will have the opportunity to cast three votes for the issues most important to him or her. Once there has been sufficient input we can discuss the issues intelligently and put forth a platform for each issue that supports and retains the integrity of our Declaration of Independence and Constitution.

I hope that each person who decides to participate will also register as an *Independent Voter*, but that will not be a requirement for membership. What will be expected is that those who wish to contribute do so intelligently and without any name-calling or insults. We have had more than enough of that already. I will do this from the web site UNITE AMERICA NOW

One of the primary functions of UNITE AMERICA NOW will be to educate the American people, and to offer a forum where every adult, no matter their race, sexual preference, or religion can express their ideas and opinions. Then we can decide on the vital issues, debate the pros and cons, and provide a platform that puts America first. The web address is www.uniteamericanow.com. There is a $10 fee to become an American Eagle Member for two years, which will include a monthly newsletter via email. The site will also offer frequently updated news stories relevant to our goal of liberty and preserving the Constitution, as well as links to those sites that share similar values.

The ultimate goal is to get as many Americans as possible to register as *Independent Voters*. Once that happens, the politicians will ignore us at their political peril. Since they will no longer be able to simply divide us into Red or Blue states and then forget about us, they will have to listen to our voice. And our opportunity to be heard will only be limited by our ability to articulate the ideas and issues most dear to our hearts.

I am reminded of a statement by JFK on February 26, 1962: "For a nation that is afraid to let its people judge the truth or falsehood in an open market is a nation that is afraid of its people."

The power-hungry addicts that prowl Washington D.C. are playing musical chairs with our future, and we can no longer count on the news media to be our only source of information. We have nothing to lose by this noble effort, and much to gain. Let us conduct our government the way most of us already conduct our personal and business lives. Let us learn to pay for the services we need, as we need them. Let us strive to understand the very special gift given to us by our Founding Fathers. Let us give thanks daily for the gift that is America. Let us commit our hearts and our minds to leaving our children the best and the brightest that America has to offer. Let us continue to be a role model for the rest of world, not by bribery or force, but by our example.

We the people are part of the greatest Republic that has ever existed. The Declaration of Independence and the Constitution were more of a beginning than an ending. They are our heritage, and we need to preserve and protect them. Only by uniting can we overcome the forces oppressing the spirit of liberty. We have survived and prospered in spite of our government and its many mistakes, but we are in danger of becoming extinct. We can stand together, or we can let the politics of fear, anger, hate, and greed tear us apart and plow asunder the great potential that is the United States of America.

We are the most creative, productive, hardworking, kind, generous people this world has ever known. We don't have to roll over and play dead anymore. We need to take back our government from the power addicts and run this nation the way our Founding Fathers intended. We the people need to build an America that will make them proud.

There is one more chapter in this book, and you can read it at our web site and help us to begin a new era in the great American Dream. As an American Eagle Member you will be able to send in your personal story, sharing how you have realized the American Dream. Our goal will be to spread the word to all of our families and loved ones, ensuring that the American Dream lives on for our children and all future Americans. Please join me on this quest at www.uniteamericanow.com.